Advance P
Entrepreneu

Entrepreneurial Trinity is a must-read for any entrepreneur looking to start and grow a successful business while maintaining a strong family and faith life. Through their honest and relatable storytelling, Brian and Mary Jo Sullivan provide invaluable wisdom and practical advice on navigating the challenges of entrepreneurship. This book will inspire you to pursue your business dreams without sacrificing what matters most.

—Mark ODonnell
Visionary at EOS Worldwide

Brian and Mary Jo's journey offers invaluable insights for any entrepreneurs balancing family, faith, and business. Their book is a compelling guide based on lived experience that inspires positive action and showcases very real-life challenges and triumphs. Key takeaways include the importance of intentionality, the necessity of sacrifice, and maintaining mental, physical, and spiritual well-being. Their narratives encourage proactive steps in building a supportive network both at home, work, and community, embracing humility, and staying true to one's core values. *Entrepreneurial Trinity* is a must-read for any faith-driven entrepreneur.

—Vince Fowler
Human Performance Coach at Fowler Performance Coaching

How wonderful to see love and faith deliver an uplifting story that touches your heart and soul. Brian, with the magic of Mary Jo, brought his expertise in the façade to reach our cores and transform our hearts. Please read this book more than once; it is going to change your life. I can't wait to see the movie!

—Dr. Moujalli Hourani
Director of Graduate Programs, Manhattan College

In a world where the essence of entrepreneurship is often masked by the allure of instant success and superficial metrics, Brian Sullivan's *Entrepreneurial Trinity* emerges as a beacon of authenticity, integrity, and profound wisdom. Brian, a man of exceptional character and a dear friend, offers not just a blueprint for business but a manifesto for life that is both deeply personal and universally applicable. I personally know this because I have known Brian and personally worked with him for a decade.

Brian's journey, as chronicled in his book, is a testament to the power of faith, the strength found in partnership, and the courage to pursue one's dreams against all odds. His narrative is punctuated with moments of vulnerability, demonstrating that true strength lies in the acknowledgment of our struggles and the resilience to overcome them. The anecdotes shared, particularly those involving his rock, Mary Jo, are poignant reminders of the indispensable role of support and love in navigating the tumultuous waters of entrepreneurship.

Entrepreneurial Trinity is more than a book; it's a reflection of Brian's heart and soul. His humility, despite immense success, and his commitment to giving back resonate throughout the pages, inspiring readers to strive for success without losing sight of what truly matters. Brian's life story, enriched by his faith and dedication to family, offers invaluable lessons on perseverance, integrity, and the transformative power of love and support.

To those embarking on their entrepreneurial journey, those in the midst of it, and even those who have reached their destination, *Entrepreneurial Trinity* is a must-read. Brian Sullivan, through his trials and triumphs, encourages us all to pursue our passions with humility, to lean on our own "rocks" during challenging times, and to always keep faith at the center of our endeavors.

Endorsing *Entrepreneurial Trinity* is an honor. Brian's journey inspires me to approach business and life with a greater sense of purpose, empathy, and generosity. His story is a vivid reminder that the true essence of entrepreneurship lies in the impact we have on the lives of others and the legacy we leave behind.

—Joe Apfelbaum
CEO of Ajax Union

ENTREPRENEURIAL TRINITY

Start and Grow a Business,
Build a Strong Family,
Nurture an Abundant Faith

ENTREPRENEURIAL TRINITY

Start and Grow a Business,
Build a Strong Family,
Nurture an Abundant Faith

BRIAN & MARY JO SULLIVAN

Printed in the United States of America

Published by Ethos Collective™
PO Box 43, Powell, OH 43065
www.ethoscollective.vip

LCCN: 2023922323
Paperback ISBN: 978-1-63680-238-1
Hardcover ISBN: 978-1-63680-239-8
e-book ISBN: 978-1-63680-240-4

Available in paperback, hardcover, e-book, and audiobook.

DEDICATION

For our four amazing parents, who taught us through their unconditional love for each other and others that in God, all things are possible. And for our seven Sullivan wonders, who teach us every day that true love in His name has no boundaries.

TABLE OF CONTENTS

NOTE TO THE READER

Our witness is Jesus Christ, the power of our witness is the Holy Spirit, and the validity of our witness will be shown in how we live our lives.

—Matt Bell

Writing this book, even just committing to writing it, was a huge stretch outside of our comfort zone. Truthfully, Mary Jo's more than mine, but it was still a stretch for both of us.

We'll share a little personal background simply because, as we all know, our history informs our decision-making processes. So, as you better understand some of our history, you can gain some clarity on the decisions we made along the way, both good and not-so-good, and gain insight into how your past may guide your decisions. You can identify similarities and differences. We were far from business experts; we just worked hard and worked together.

As I think back over the past fourteen years, I'm incredibly grateful that I was naive to what the future would hold. Had I known some of the early struggles, Mary Jo and I might not have gone down this great road. Now that we are on the other side of selling and exiting the business that we started in 2010, we are so blessed that we decided to start our entrepreneurial journey when we did.

Often, Mary Jo and I look back over the last few decades and realize we learned most of our lessons the hard way. And when we do, we feel a passion for helping those embarking on the entrepreneurial adventure. While we learned many lessons through trial and error, we were also blessed to learn many lessons from extraordinary individuals through books, podcasts, coaching programs, mentors, and entrepreneurial friends.

We simply wanted to share our journey of starting, building, and selling our company while simultaneously growing our family and strengthening our faith. We don't pretend that all our decisions were right or wrong. But we hope you might gain some insight or pull a lesson or two from our stories, things we wish we knew when we started this journey. So we decided to write this book as if you, the reader, are our thirty-five-year-old selves.

Mary Jo and I chose the image of the Trinity for this book because we learned that all three components must be strong and support each other. If one aspect struggled, it would quickly impact the other two. When I was dealing with any tough business decision, the more I leaned on the grounding of my faith and the support of my family, the better the outcome. Similarly, the success of the business blessed our family and strengthened our faith.

We feel blessed to have arrived where we are now in our journey to raise a family, grow our faith, and create a successful business. We know that success is measured differently by everyone. While we are well aware that we could've had more success in each aspect of the Entrepreneurial Trinity, we certainly could've had much less.

Use our examples to learn from our mistakes and build on our knowledge. Don't let the setbacks discourage you. You can do it. We believe in you. And, in the words of Mary Jo, "You've got this. You're almost there." We'll be rooting for you and, more importantly, praying for you. We'll be here if you need us.

INTRODUCTION

...lead a life worthy of the calling to which you have been called, with all humility and gentleness, with patience, bearing with one another in love, making every effort to maintain the unity of the Spirit in the bond of peace.

—Ephesians 4:1-3

I was sitting on the couch one late night in the Fall of 2010, head down on the laptop. I had come home from the office in time to see the kids before they went to bed, as I tried to do two or three nights per week and then poured myself back into work. Mary Jo must've known something was up by my body language because as she headed up to bed, she was a little more persistent than normal.

"Why don't you come to bed too?" she said.

I responded that I'd be up soon; I just had to get something done.

She pushed back. "What are you working on?"

I replied, "It's nothing. I won't stay up too late."

She knew I was lying. When she pushed back again, I told her the truth: I was working on my resume.

Six months into the business, I felt that I was failing in business but more so at home and in my faith. Our savings were steadily approaching zero. I was working 100+ hours per week and not putting nearly enough time into my family and my faith. She very calmly walked over, closed the laptop, and said, "You've got this; you're almost there." She suggested that I get a good night's sleep, stay home to see the kids when they wake up in the morning, and go into the office refreshed.

Mary Jo's wisdom was spot on. I was exhausted and frustrated, but most of all, I was insecure, and her words of confidence in me were exactly what I needed to press on.

Within a few weeks, we landed our first project and, a few months after that, started turning a profit. The rest, as they say, is history. If not for her confidence in me, we would have a very different story. Now, to be clear, it wasn't blind faith. She likely had heard me speak of potential opportunities, and she knew we were almost there. But at that time, I couldn't see it—thank God she could.

Mary Jo had always been my rock, and once again, she was right. Mary Jo believed in me when I didn't have enough confidence left to believe in myself. Starting a business and putting in the hours required to make it real is difficult. She carried the bulk of our family burden in those early years. Her gracious attitude and support meant that our marriage grew stronger during a phase of business that drives many couples apart.

Who is your rock?

As you navigate your entrepreneurial journey, it's important to have someone who has your back and will tell you the truth. For many people, that is their spouse, but for others, it isn't. I have a good friend whose father is his business rock. Just know who your rock is.

Dear Brian,

Although you were only a mere six months into your entrepreneurial journey, you had put an incredible amount of stress upon yourself. I know your six-month vision for the business was proving to be a different reality thus far. You were working a tremendous amount of hours and had tried to make a point each evening to call the kids from the office to speak to them before they would go off to bed. This had become the routine since most nights, you were getting home well after they and I had gone to sleep. I had started to develop a jealousy for the business.

The days were long with three toddlers, and some nights, I just wished you were home to help at bath time or the post-dinner tornado clean-up. When we would speak briefly on the phone when you would call in the evenings, you would sometimes pick up on my frustrations. You'd even ask on occasion, "Do you want me to come home and help?" I'd always say no even though I wanted to say yes, and I think there was a part of you that wanted me to say yes. But we both knew, through the exhaustion and through the frustrations, this was part of the sacrifice and early struggles of starting a business.

This one particular night, you came home earlier than usual, home in time to have dinner with me and the kids. When you were present, you were always "present." You read them their books, tucked them in, said prayers with them, and kissed the three of them good night. I've heard you tell the story of this night over the past 14 years more times than I can count. But each time you tell it, I can't help but thank our Lord. It was not my words or my strength or my wisdom that closed your laptop; it was His grace. It was the grace of God that opened my eyes and my heart to your short-term struggle as you were working on the couch that night.

There is no doubt in my mind that had I not intervened, a good night's sleep would have brought you to the same conclusion on your own. But God let us have our first entrepreneurial moment as a couple right there in our living room that night. It had only been six months, after all! God reminded me I married a born leader who had everything he needed to get this business up and going. He also reminded me He had my back to be the loving, strong, and supportive wife that you needed to succeed.

I love you,
MJ

Hey Mary Jo,

As I think back over the past 20 years of our marriage, but especially the past 14 years since starting the business, I can't help but realize how much our marriage vows have meant to us. The words we said over two decades ago when the two of us became one: "I promise to be true to you in good times and in bad, in sickness and in health. I will love you and honor you all the days of my life," were sure put to the test.

Sure, we meant it when we said those vows, but we really had no idea what we were signing up for—thank God, the Good Lord did. The roller coaster of good times and bad was a children's coaster prior to starting the business in comparison to after, but just like any great roller coaster, any great business, and any great marriage, the good times far outweigh the bad.

The words in sickness and in health have reverberated more so for those around us, not necessarily the two of us directly, but together, acting as one, we have been able to tackle more challenges than we could've imagined way back then.

There's no doubt in my mind that our faith in God has helped us through all the blessings and challenges, as well as our commitment to those vows that we said in His house before God and our families.

Love,
Brian

I

CONCEPTION

Trust in the Lord with all your heart, and do not rely on your own insight. In all your ways, acknowledge Him, and He will make straight your paths.

—Proverbs 3:5-6

Similar to starting a family, it was important for us to know our motivation and our why when starting the business. As peaks and valleys arrived, and they did, remembering our motivation helped us stay the course. We planned to the extent that we were comfortable, but as they say, we make plans, and God laughs. Keeping our eye on the motivation helped us laugh along with Him while placing all our trust in Him.

Motivation and Inspiration

I was very fortunate to be the son of Pat and Peggy Sullivan and have two wonderful sisters. My parents both emigrated from Ireland as young adults. My mother came in 1959 and my father in 1960, both at the age of 20. Although they came to New York separately and met here, they were from the same county in Ireland. Both were from very hardworking families, and both started working very young, my dad on his family farm, my mother in a hotel in town.

When they immigrated to New York, they felt one of their responsibilities was to help support their families back home in Ireland. At a young age, I remember learning about the support they provided their families back home and being incredibly impressed by their loyalty and their ability to make every dollar count for the benefit of their family. My sisters and I were blessed to grow up in a very loving home.

My parents worked very hard but were there for us whenever we needed them. My dad worked for an electric utility company, Con Edison, not too far from home. When we were young, my mother worked nights and weekends as a waitress, but as we started to get older, she didn't work outside the home and spent the time nurturing our young family. When I entered middle school, she went back to work in the cafeteria of a local public school.

They worked very hard to be able to send us to private Catholic schools because they felt that was where we would get the best well-rounded education in line with their values. Similarly, they sacrificed very hard to purchase a house in Whitestone, a nice town in Queens, New York, with a very suburban feel.

It was really a great place to grow up, and it was probably a stretch for them when they bought their house there. But again, they recognized the value in making that investment.

I was also fortunate that they stretched every dollar to make it count and were willing to invest not only in a private Catholic high school but also in private Catholic colleges for me and my sisters. Although we had some student loan debt, it was certainly very modest compared to some of my peers.

As you may be able to tell, they have been and still are an unbelievable motivation and inspiration for me, my wife, and our kids as well as my sisters and their families. I share all of that with you because you may want to look at your parents or other families for motivation and inspiration. Be sure to keep them in mind—what they've been through and what they've accomplished. When we hit our low points, we can feel alone. For me, knowing that people "just like me" accomplished much more than I was currently trying to accomplish brought great comfort.

Outgrowing Insecurities

Growing up in the early eighties looking like Ralphie from *A Christmas Story*, complete with big thick glasses, made for some pretty tough encounters in the schoolyard and created some deep insecurities that I still battle today. But it also created some mental toughness and a growing lack of concern for what random people think of me.

As I grew out of the "Ralphie phase" through high school and college, my insecurities started to decrease, bolstered by the support of some tremendous individuals that I was blessed to meet along the way. The high school I attended, St. Francis Prep, was a very large school that allowed me the opportunity to slowly navigate through finding my friends and exploring different clubs and interests while enjoying some anonymity, at least early on. From Prep, I moved on to Manhattan College, a small college in the Bronx known for its Catholic traditions and its strong School of Engineering.

The environment in Manhattan really allowed me to come out of my shell, sometimes too much. The genuine concern from many of the students and faculty was a godsend for me as I navigated my four years of college and developed into an adult. As a result of the relative freedom of college life (a.k.a. partying) and the opportunities to get involved in different activities and clubs, I was spreading myself very thin socially and not putting the proper effort into my classwork. As such, I was constantly playing catch up and struggled academically in my freshman and sophomore years. This led to some really, really low points in my self-confidence. Fortunately, my family, friends, and some key faculty members had more faith in me than I did, so I pushed through and found my groove.

Sarai

Inspired by my sister Patricia's mission trip while attending Fairfield University, I decided to sign up for a mission trip to Honduras in my junior year at Manhattan College. In 1996, I made my first of two trips to San Pedro Sula, Honduras. To say those trips had a huge impact on my life is a massive understatement. Before the first trip, I was talking to a friend who had been there the year before. He told me about a young girl named Sarai, whom he had met in an orphanage while he was there. She had touched his heart, and he told me to make sure I found her when I was there.

During my first trip, we spent our days building a home for a 17-year-old girl who was raising her four siblings and her own baby alone because her parents had both died of AIDS. The physical exhaustion of building in the heat in Honduras always wiped us out. However, as soon as we walked in the gate of the orphanage run by the School Sisters of Notre Dame each night, the exhaustion quickly dissipated when we saw these beautiful young kids running towards us. These children had very little material possessions but were so incredibly happy. The head nun at the orphanage, Hermana Teresa, was a petite, sweet woman. Yet, she managed to protect all of these beautiful children from the outside elements. There, I, too, was drawn to the beautiful little Honduran princess, Sarai. She had my heart instantly. The thought of her energy and infectious smile is something that still warms my heart to this day.

When we left to go home from that first trip, we were all emotional. I was crying as I left Sarai and vowed to come back and see her again. My friend Tom was also quite emotional after leaving. I found out that a little boy he had been friendly with all week had given him his second-grade school certificate. Tom was so gracious for this certificate and asked the young boy why he wanted to give it to him. His answer was because it was the only possession that he had, and he wanted Tom to have it. Man, we all lost it. What a spirit of gratitude and a heart of giving these wonderful children have.

So, needless to say, in my senior year, I went back for another trip to Honduras. I was so excited to go again to help and see the beautiful children, but especially to see my Sarai. When we went to the orphanage the first day, I was crushed to learn that she had been moved to another orphanage in another town that had a school that she could attend. A few days later, beautiful Hermana Teresa let me know that she was headed to that orphanage and invited me to join her. When we arrived, Sarai was in school. So, the team that ran that orphanage sent for her and brought her home to see me. As she walked into the long driveway, I could see that she was justifiably nervous. And at six years old, I assumed she didn't remember me. As she got closer, however, she started walking faster and eventually ran to me.

I hugged her with everything I had. And then we sat and talked. My Spanish is terrible, but the beauty of kids is that they will find a way to communicate. They don't care that we can't speak the same language. They figure it out. She was sitting on my lap and, after a while, said, "Bop, bop, bop." She remembered that on that first trip, I used to bounce her on my knee and say, "Bop, bop, bop." I had forgotten that. But she did not. Yeah, I started crying immediately.

I left that day knowing that one day, I would adopt internationally. That trip, that beautiful little face, changed my life. I love you, Sarai. Thank you, wherever you are. I think of you all the time.

LeeAnn

When I landed my first internship, it was the first time I realized I could probably hold my own in the real world. I was fortunate to intern and then eventually land my first job with a second-generation family-owned construction company. Through observing and, at times, working alongside the leadership there, I began to dream about one day owning/running my own company. I still struggled with the full confidence that I could do it, but at least I allowed myself to dream.

While at that company, I had the opportunity to travel to Baltimore for a one-year project and then to Greenville, South Carolina, the following year. A team of us worked on both projects together. Construction can be rough, gruff, and stressful, no doubt. Many times, the loudest, most assertive voice wins, not necessarily the one who's right. That was not an environment that I was well suited for, and it weighed on me. It apparently changed me, too, so much that one of the women on our team who worked on both projects asked me to speak to her one day.

LeeAnn, very compassionately and clearly nervous, shared with me that I had changed. I was not the same person who started on the first project in Baltimore. And it was clear that wasn't a compliment. She gently urged me to think about her words and the impact working in this environment was having on me.

I certainly did think about it. I lie awake for several nights thinking about it. Eventually, I realized that I needed to change where I worked to get back to the person that I wanted to be. Thank you, LeeAnn. God bless you.

It took a lot of courage for her to share that with me, as well as a great deal of compassion and care as a friend, to push herself outside of her comfort zone. For that, I'm incredibly grateful. It actually made me realize that I needed to be that courageous for people I love moving forward. It can be very difficult to have conversations like that. But if we truly love and care for the people around us, we need to be that courageous. We need more LeeAnn's in this world.

Have you been a LeeAnn for someone? Are you courageous enough to push yourself outside your comfort zone to help someone you care for be their best?

After a few years on the construction side of the engineering industry, I decided to switch and work for an engineering firm. I worked for a firm whose founder still ran the business. Observing what he was able to do for his family and those around him is what further ignited the fire in me to one day start my own firm.

Additionally, as part of this team, I started to grow as an engineer and as a leader. As I gained confidence in who I was professionally, it led to increased confidence personally, and I gained the courage to shoot my shot with a close family friend, Mary Jo. We grew up on the same street, our families were very close friends, and I had a big crush on her for as long as I can remember and still do.

Dear Brian.

It was a beautiful spring evening, the Thursday before Memorial Day Weekend, to be exact. I said bye to Pop, opened the screen door to my parent's house, and started my run down Cryders Lane. I made it to the Throgs Neck Bridge and turned onto the dirt path. I was approaching the baseball fields under the bridge, and there you were, standing shoulder to shoulder with your Dad, watching a little league game. I heard from your sister Eileen that you were thinking of moving back home. You had been living down south for years, working for a construction company following your graduation from Manhattan College.

Was I insane to think that just maybe you were coming back for me? You gave me a great hug, as you always did when I approached you and your Dad standing there.

We were both born and raised on 155th Street in Whitestone, New York, with only eight houses separating our two homes. We spent summers running up and down that block: manhunt, wiffle ball, running bases, ice cream from Steve the ice cream man, big wheels races, swimming in each other's pools. Rama family parties were never complete unless "The Sullivans" were there. Following my college graduation, I left for Haiti—my heart was calling me to volunteer for a year as a nurse in Fr. Rick Frechette's Pere Damien Hospital, a pediatric hospital in Petionville, Haiti.

To this day, I remember Mr. Russo, my amazing philosophy teacher at Molloy College, encouraging the class to take a year following graduation to go volunteer somewhere. I thought I could do that; I want to do that! I returned to New York after my year in Haiti, and you had left for down south to go work following your graduation. We would run into each other from time to time during our early 20s; something just felt so right every time I would see you. It was never easy to see your car drive past my house and head back down South. I knew God had a plan for me; I just prayed so hard it included you.

Standing there with you and your dad under the Throgs Neck Bridge, you asked me, "Are you going up to the Catskills this weekend?" Memorial Day weekends up in the Catskills for the Irish Festival had become a long-standing tradition with all of our friends. But this particular weekend, God had an agenda, and He was making it known. We spent the weekend with family and friends, dancing to Irish bands, just having the time of our lives.

I remember that Friday night when the two of us stayed up talking after everyone had gone to bed. You told me you were moving back to New York and asked me if I knew why. I think we both knew at that moment what was happening. We had both spent years after college carving our own paths, attempting to make the best versions of ourselves. If God was going to bring us together, it was going to be on His terms, and that it was.

I loved you for years, but I couldn't believe God would ever think I was worthy of your love, worthy of someone like you. You are a saint and a gift, and I vowed that night never to take that for granted. That Tuesday, you were in your car heading down to South Carolina to pack up all your things and move back to New York.

We never looked back after that weekend; we started dating immediately, and on August 23, 2003, in St. Luke's Church in Whitestone, NY, with God present, we went from eight houses apart to husband and wife under one roof!

I love you,
MJ

In the years following my college graduation, I accumulated a decent amount of debt on dumb purchases, including a brand new car, of which the high payments were only outweighed by the high cost of the insurance, a new apartment, and a social life to match. As I started to mature, and as soon as Mary Jo and I began dating, I realized that I had to be more responsible and get control of my debt.

While Mary Jo and I were in Florida visiting her parents, I walked into a bookstore, and right up front was a table display for Dave Ramsey's book, *Total Money Makeover*. It's one of those vivid memories I have. I can still picture the table in my mind; I can still picture the cover of the 100 books stacked up and Dave's smiling face looking back. Something about the book, something about that point in my life, just grabbed me.

I picked it up, read the back cover, and knew that this was for me. I purchased the book and immediately started reading it, and more importantly, I immediately started implementing his 7 Baby Steps to get out of debt. While, in hindsight, the debt was relatively small, it was enough that I felt the weight of it for years to come. So much so that when Mary Jo and I got engaged on a beautiful trip to Niagara Falls, a great memory was clouded because I constantly had on my mind that I had yet to share with her that I had this debt.

I felt so foolish for having it. I felt ashamed, really, and thought that she would not want to be married to someone so foolish. So, on the way home from Niagara Falls after I had proposed, I let her know about the debt. Her reaction was a blessing. She said, "No problem." I remember telling her this long, convoluted description and rushing through something really fast. And she just kind of looked at me like, okay, we'll get through it. That was one early sign that she was fully committed to working together as a team to conquer whatever life throws our way.

And we did get through it. I worked through the baby steps and paid off all the debt, and we went into our marriage debt-free and in a really good spot.

The mental impact of having that debt and feeling ashamed turned out to be a blessing for me for years to come. Mary Jo and I never believed in accumulating debt from then on. So we paid cash for everything—for used cars, for our nights out, and for any trips we went on. Nothing went on a credit card.

Dear Brian,

I remember the moment crystal clear soon after we got engaged when you told me about the debt you had accumulated after you finished college. It was minimal debt in my mind, but I could see how much this was weighing on you. I loved how upfront and honest you needed to be with me. If there was a moment that set us up to be a successful entrepreneurial couple, this was it.

I remember you speaking to me about Dave's book, Total Money Makeover. I loved Dave's philosophies, and I was totally on board with starting our marriage using them. Now, truth be told, when you broke out the charts and Excel spreadsheets one evening before we were even married, I thought to myself, dear Lord, what have I gotten myself into? But all kidding aside, we both had heard stories about financial insecurity and financial stress destroying marriages. I was grateful to God for putting us in that bookstore down in Florida and for you feeling compelled to pick up and purchase Dave's book that day.

Truth be told, soon after we started implementing Dave's budget suggestions and your spreadsheets kept coming, I contemplated purchasing a "Dave Ramsey ruined my life" T-shirt, which is a real thing, apparently. But in all honesty, the positive impact that book and your immediate honesty about your debt early on in our relationship had on our lives is immeasurable.

We made a commitment to our marriage right then and there that we were going to build our marriage on a financially strong foundation. I thank our Lord that you are such a man of integrity and that keeping that amount of debt away from me after our engagement weighed on your heart. You made a decision to confront me with something you were obviously very embarrassed about. I wish that, as you struggled that day to get the words out, you only knew the impact that conversation would have on us as a couple and our marriage.

You set the tone and foundation that a marriage built on faith, honesty, transparency, and fiscal responsibility is built to last. I love this quote from Dave, and it just sums up our journey beautifully! "Debt is normal. But the truth is that you should not want to be normal. You need to be willing to be weird. Weird is when you live sacrificially in the present, pay off your past, and invest in a financially peaceful future." Brian, thank you for being your strong, humbly confident self and always embracing your "weird."

I love you!
MJ

I became a big Dave Ramsey fan and listened to his podcasts almost every day. The people he interviewed and the stories he shared about getting through their debt snowball are so inspiring and motivating. He also had all sorts of different guests. One day, he interviewed his friend Dan Miller, who wrote the book *48 Days to the Work You Love*, which, as the title implies, provided wisdom, guidance, and motivation to find work they love, often as an entrepreneur.

Dan also had a weekly podcast where he shared many stories of people who have done the same. Dan was a soft-spoken Southern gentleman with incalculable wisdom. Through Dan's content, I gained the confidence and courage to one day start my own business.

Sadly, Dan went home to the Lord on January 21, 2024, and in true Dan Miller style, his final podcast on December 29, 2023, was beautiful, incredibly courageous, inspiring, and a true reflection of what he preached. He often instructed us to "never let your circumstances determine your attitude," and wow, did he live that out in his final days.

Dave and Dan had a tremendous impact on our entrepreneurial journey. The fact that they did it through books and podcasts, without ever having met us, is indicative of the power of others sharing their journey. "People learn from one another just as iron sharpens iron" (Proverbs 27:17). Sometimes, we need to pick up some wisdom from others. Sometimes, we need to pick up a little courage from others. And sometimes, we need both. Fortunately, Dan and Dave were both for us.

Who are the authors, mentors, and influencers that you are plugged into and gaining wisdom from?

Hey Mary Jo,

Since we started the business, I can't tell you how many times I've heard the word "courage" mentioned in a reading at church, as well as similar phrases like "do not be afraid." At first, I thought it was just because I was attuned to it, as it seemed to take more and more courage every day to keep chugging along.

Courage is a virtue that I believe is contagious. Benefiting from the courage of others has directly strengthened my resolve to be courageous for the benefit of others. When those benefits are realized, my resolve intensifies to do it again and again in even bigger ways.

Today's world needs courageous men and women. I suppose that's true of the past and the future as well, which is why the theme is repeated literally hundreds of times in the Bible. Courage is a timeless principle that never goes out of style.

There are many extraordinary examples of courage in the Bible that are not likely for any of us to have to live up to: Jesus dying on the cross; Mary laying witness to it; Moses leading the Israelites out of Egypt; Padre Pio embracing the stigmata . . . the list goes on and on.

Nevertheless, comparatively smaller acts of courage still require a strong resolve as well as a deep faith in God and His vision. Today's conventional wisdom says that you can't mix business and faith; however, I have many friends who run their businesses while not shying away from their faith. In fact, they proudly display and discuss their Christian, Jewish, or Islamic beliefs.

Some may believe that this has a negative impact on their business, but I am a firm believer that it helps tremendously. Especially when done with an inclusive mindset rather than excluding others; this was how Jesus showed us how to live. He had the courage to follow God's plan for his life regardless of how trying and difficult the road ahead was and without fully knowing where that road would lead.

"Yet not as I will, but as you will . . . may your will be done" were his famous words to God. It's been my observation that if we embrace God's will for our lives and our businesses, we will be much happier, much more successful, and, more importantly, much more impactful.

Love,
Brian

II
NEWBORN

The world needs witnesses more than it does teachers.

—Pope Paul VI

Once the business has been planned out—conceived—it's time to birth the idea. A new business is like a newborn child in many ways: it requires constant attention, devotion, and care. Like a child, what you put into a new business sets the direction of its life. This includes the people you hire, who you choose to do business with, and how you decide to run your business.

Security Blanket

When we made the decision to start the business, I was trepidatious because we had three small kids at home; however, Mary Jo was much more pragmatic. She said, "Now is the time. If we don't go on vacation and if we have to eat rice and beans every day, the kids won't know. If we have to pause the kids' college funds, we'll have the time to catch up." That was the final discussion. From there on, it wasn't if we would start the business; it was how quickly could we start.

I recognize that when we had a small, growing family and decided to leave a relatively secure job and take the risk, or perceived risk, of starting our engineering firm, we did so with the security blanket of knowing that our parents would have done anything for us. That meant letting us move back into their house if we needed to. I can assure you that fear crossed my mind many times in the early years of the business. We recognize that many people don't have that luxury, and we were very blessed to have that.

Knowing what the absolute worst-case scenario would be if the business had failed was really critical for us when we decided to make the leap. And then even more critical, one year later, when the business was still struggling to get on its feet.

When I first told my parents I was leaving my relatively stable job to take the leap as an entrepreneur for our family, I remember the look of excitement, as well as the look of concern on their faces. Rightfully, as parents, they were worried for their son, daughter-in-law, and their grandchildren. After all, they had chosen to take relatively secure jobs for the stability of their family, which was likely impacted by the difficult job opportunities in their home country of Ireland at the time they left.

Back then, I didn't recognize where their worry came from. I thought it was a lack of confidence. In hindsight, it was a normal parental concern, especially based on their emigrant history. The risk that they took leaving Ireland and all that was familiar to them far outweighs any entrepreneurial risk that we took. They certainly had the "do whatever it takes" attitude that Brian Buffini attributes to the success of many immigrants.[1] In reality, they embodied all seven of the key characteristics that he defines.

Conversely, years later, seeing the look of relief and joy, as well as maybe a little pride on my parents' faces when I told them that I was selling the business, is a moment I'll treasure forever. As a parent, I now fully understand why they felt those worrisome emotions early on.

What is the realistic, worst-case scenario if your business doesn't succeed as you envision? Taking into account the word realistic, it's not as bad as we'd otherwise imagine, right?

Dear Brian,

We were so fortunate at the time you and I decided "now" would be a good time for you to launch your own engineering firm that I was working at Memorial Sloan Kettering. I had been there eight years at the time of the business's birth, and they had just been so extremely wonderful to me, not to mention it was an incredibly rewarding place to work. I have always been so grateful to your sister, Eileen, for encouraging me to apply for a job at MSKCC's Pediatric Day Hospital. My nurse manager always got a kick out of telling me the story of how Eileen, who was working in Sloan's nuclear medicine department at the time, came up onto the PDH unit and, in the sweetest way possible, said, "This is my sister-in-law's resume. You need to hire her. You'll love her." What an amazing sister-in-law to stick her neck out for me like that!

When we started the business, I was only working two ten-hour days a week. Maintaining the 20 hours a week allowed us to continue full medical benefits for the entire family through the hospital, and this gave us both such relief while the business was getting off the ground. I loved working two days a week; it was a perfect balance. I was home with the kids the majority of the week, but I also still got to work as a pediatric nurse for those two days, something I truly adored and was blessed to do.

My mom, who lived with us, and your parents were pivotal in helping with the kids. Our kids never spent a day in daycare. They were always home on the days we were both working—what a blessing. Your hours were insane at the time, and on the days I went into Manhattan, I needed to leave the house by 5:15 in the morning. Your parents, who were living in Queens at the time, would wake up at 3:30 a.m., drive out to New Jersey in the complete dark, and be out to our house before I left at 5:15. They'd show up at our door with the biggest smiles on their faces, ready to jump into action with whichever toddler or infant was awake upon their arrival.

There were numerous occasions I'd be leaving them with a child who had a fever, runny nose, a stomach bug, teething, ear infection, or just plain cranky, and nothing ever phased them. It was funny; both our moms had the same expression as I'd be running out the door in the morning, apologizing to them for leaving them with the mess or a screaming child. They'd both put their hands up in this extremely calm manner and say, "We'll be fine. We'll get through the day." My God, what a blessing they were to us.

This went on for a few years. Your parents were out from Queens for a day or two at our house, then up two blocks to your sister Eileen's house for two days, and then up to Goshen, NY, to your sister Patricia's house to help out there. To say your parents are extraordinary is a complete understatement.

They are two of the most selfless people I have yet to meet in my life. I remember the joy in their voices when they would describe their typical week to one of our neighbors or friends. They spent the largest part of their retirement traveling all over the tri-state area, watching their grandkids, and if you asked them, they'd tell you one faster than the other; they wouldn't have had it any other way. Brian, I can't help but think of the beautiful toast your sister Patricia gave at your parent's 50th wedding anniversary celebration in Ireland. She said, "They show up; they are always present," and this was the utmost truth. No matter the circumstances, they showed up. What a gift and blessing.

Your parents and my mom were instrumental in the business's early success. I often think that if it were not for them, I would have never been able to work as long as I did at MSKCC with the hours you were keeping. They alleviated a tremendous amount of stress, which would have easily accumulated and, quite possibly, made us doubt our decision to start the business when we did. I do not know what we would have done without them!

I love you,
MJ

Understanding What Success Looks Like

One of the most important things I believe an entrepreneurial couple can do when starting any business is to identify what success looks like for them. Success is measured in many, many different ways, and the only ways that matter are those of that couple specifically.

Some of my really good friends from college started very similar engineering firms to mine, one well before mine and one right around the same time. Thank God, all of us have been very successful, but in very different ways.

One is a solopreneur who's absolutely crushing it, able to control his schedule the way he wants, coaching his children's sports, attending their events in college, and juggling all of the other commitments that this fantastic dad has on his plate. All while creating a wonderful income for his family and continuing to do the work that he loves. As an engineer, he is uniquely gifted, and he loves dealing with clients as well as designing and coming up with solutions that no one else can think of.

The second has a firm with ten or so employees. So he gets the balance of still being involved in engineering while having people on his team that he can have an impact on. So he's able to perform both aspects of the business that he loves.

For me, I gave up on most of the engineering as I grew our firm to eventually a team of 50+ people. Giving up the engineering portion wasn't that difficult for me because I really love dealing with people. I love dealing with the clients and our team members, and more importantly, I love having an impact on people. Giving up the engineering portion allowed me to do that.

So, as you can see, for each of us, success is measured very differently. But all three of us are no doubt successful in our own rights. Although both of those guys could have grown their companies to have 100 or even 200 people on their teams, I admire the fact that they know what they want and are tempering the growth of their companies to achieve what success looks like for them.

What does success look like to you?

For our full recommended list of questions to ask before starting the journey, see Appendix A. However, you may want to finish the book before answering the questions. Knowing the end of our story may impact how you envision your story playing out.

Bootstrapping vs Debt

The definition of success isn't limited to the size of your business. In fact, it can be heavily dependent on your financial mindset. As mentioned in the previous chapter, Dave Ramsey and his philosophies were key to getting me and then our family to a point of financial stability and relative strength. His teachings provided enough of a foundation that we were able to take the leap of faith to start our engineering firm without knowing when, or even if, revenue would come in the door. Dave also wrote a book called *Entreleadership* about how he runs his business, which I devoured.

So, it made sense that when we started the business, we used the same "debt-free" mindset. For the first few weeks, I used a table at the local public library to do much of the initial work of launching the business from our family's Macbook. This fits well in the budget but obviously wasn't a great long-term strategy, particularly on the rare occasion that I received a phone call. I would have to quickly scramble to gather all of my items and get outside to answer the call. I looked like a whirling dervish running through the library.

Sitting in the library, I didn't let the meager surroundings dampen my optimism. I worked on some of our earliest marketing efforts and the templates that we needed to run the business. I also started working on a detailed business plan, including what it would look like each year for the next five years, then a 10-, 20-, 30-, and 40-year revenue picture. Yes, I was bold enough to set a 40-year employee count and revenue goal while sitting in a free public space.

As you may have noticed, I stated that I *started* creating a business plan in the library. The template I used for the business plan was 40+ pages and was way more detailed than I needed and had the stamina for. I'm sure that level of detail is great for some people, although for me, I went through the first ten pages or so, focusing on the high-level topics and stopped there. When I dug up the business plan several years later, I realized that going any further wouldn't have likely been productive for me because I had no idea what I was about to get into and would've likely had to change so much along the way. Being fixed to a detailed plan may not have allowed me to adjust and pivot as much as I needed to.

To that end, I was way off on the revenue and employee goals that I had set. In the first two years, I was significantly lower than the goals, and every year after that, our actual numbers far surpassed the goals that I had set.

When we did rent our first space, it was a relatively modest space made up primarily of furniture from home or damaged items purchased at a deep discount. I've often wondered how things would've been if we hadn't adopted Dave's ways in the business. It would be safe to bet that we would not have used folding tables and folding chairs as furniture for our third and fourth employees. Left to my own devices, I likely would've had brand new desks and chairs bought on credit, as well as all the typical trappings that nobody else would've ever seen.

That debt-free mindset carried into giving debit cards to all of our employees who would be traveling to job sites. This appeared to be a big risk as the money came directly out of our company's checking account, but in my mind, the clear transparency of seeing what was coming out of the checking account in real time was more beneficial than getting blindsided by a surprise on the credit card statement at the end of the month. Additionally, as Dave Ramsey discusses, the psychology of spending cash, or in this case, using a debit card instead of a credit card, has a distinct impact on our buying patterns. Since we focused on hiring the right people and spoke openly about the company's finances, this frugal purchasing philosophy passed throughout our team as well.

As the business grew, we eventually took out a line of credit to ensure that if a crisis hit—and at least one will hit any business—we would be able to cover employees' payroll. We only did this after we had the proper controls in place, thanks to Josh, our CFO, who did a great job monitoring our finances and preventing me from making any more significant dumb financial decisions.

One thing I am very confident about is that when that crisis hit, in the form of the COVID-19 pandemic, the debt-free mindset allowed us to make decisions from a position of strength. The fact that we had zero debt, 4+ months of a full emergency fund, and an untapped line of credit helped ensure that our leadership team made decisions based on facts and observations rather than fear and emotion.

First Hire: Job Offer in a Driveway

Before cash flow and debt were active concerns, I had to hire employees. I knew how to do the work my company would be doing, but there were many other required roles I had no experience doing. My mind would spin for hours about where to get quality employees and what a best-fit employee would look like.

As I talked things out with our family, our sister-in-law, Donna, expressed interest in working for the company and helping to get it off the ground. I shared with her that I'd love to have her on the team, but with no predicted revenue coming in to start the company, I wouldn't be able to hire her for a long time because I wouldn't be able to pay her. Donna's response was essentially, "Come on. I love you guys. I'll do it for free until you can afford to pay me. It will likely help you guys get started to have some office help."

Well, a few weeks later, I drove to Donna's house, asked her if she was serious, and then hired our first employee with a five-minute conversation in her driveway. Things got very real when I had someone else counting on the success of the company. I recognized the sacrifice that Donna and her husband, Vinny, Mary Jo's brother, were making in their own household to help get our business off the ground. But I knew they were confident enough in me, and that was a huge boost to my confidence *and* motivation.

On June 1, when we moved into our first office, Donna joined the team and worked, or should I say volunteered, two to three days per week for several months until I was able to pay her. Her presence, especially at the start, was tremendous. Her background as a teacher and as an English major was critical in helping me and, eventually, the other engineers learn how to communicate more effectively. Her hunger and sales expertise as a former realtor helped with the scrappy, all-hands-on-deck nature of a startup.

I've heard many stories about how working with family members can be challenging. However, Donna and I set up boundaries early regarding not discussing family issues at work and work issues with the family. She was a critical part of our business, especially for our early success.

Do you have a Donna in your support system? If not, go out and find yourself a Donna.

Dear Brian,

I'm sure you'll agree with me when I say if there was one person who had more confidence in the success of the business right out of the gates, other than the two of us, it was for sure our sister-in-law Donna. I remember talking to her one day in the front door hallway of our first house. It was super early on after you started the company, and you had rented your first office space on Valley Road.

We pieced together some furniture and folding tables from the house you could use to fill the office space, and Donna had stopped by to pick up some cleaning supplies. She wanted to give the office a quick clean before bringing some of the furniture in. I thanked her there at our front door for doing all of this for us and being such a great support to you even though things were off to a super slow start. I remember her reply being, "Are you kidding? This is going to be something special, something great, and I want to be part of it . . . but we just need the phone to ring. We just need that first call. He just needs to land that first project."

The three of us knew this was true. You were working unbelievably hard to land any project you could. Donna was our brave face, creating an office and doing anything to keep busy until that phone would eventually start to ring, and I was leaning hard on our Lord to give you the strength and hope to hang in there and show us the path He had laid out for our family. You and I knew in our hearts you were birthing something great. Donna was so right, but to have her confidence and support in those early days was pivotal to both of us.

I love you,
MJ

First Head of Household

While hiring a family member had unique benefits and challenges, things with Donna went smoothly. From the early days, sitting in the library drafting my 40-year vision, I knew we needed a bigger team to achieve my goals. I spent a lot of time thinking about the most critical roles to hire first and what values I wanted my team to share.

As I prepared for my first technical hire, I knew that I had to hire someone whom I could trust implicitly to do what he said he would do and who had technical expertise. I also knew that I needed someone who would be scrappy and a hard worker. Most of all, it needed to be someone I liked.

Alan and I had worked together previously. Alan had since moved out of the New York area and was working for a national contractor. One day, he came to visit me in the office. We had a very open, honest discussion based on the trust we had previously built—Alan checked all the boxes of an ideal hire. I spoke to him about the opportunity, and thankfully, he agreed to join.

Because of our open, honest dialogue, I knew throughout his tenure with us that Alan was thinking of moving out of the New York area. So, eventually, years later, when he decided to relocate his family, I knew well in advance and was able to set our team up for a successful transition. Similarly, Alan was able to comfortably look for a new opportunity and a new place to live while continuing to work with our team. That open, honest dialogue continued after he left, and fortunately, Alan rejoined our team several years later.

Open, honest conversations are incredibly important in business. They require vulnerability from both sides and trust that sharing information will not be used against the other party. If done correctly, they are incredibly beneficial. Had we not had such an open, honest dialogue, I might not have known that Alan was going to move until the required two weeks' notice. And then I would have had to scramble to find somebody to replace him. Similarly, he would have had a hard time disguising his search for a new opportunity while working with our team. Open, honest communication has been a blessing to our team substantially more than it has hurt.

In addition to being our first hire with experience in our niche, Alan was also our first hire who was a head of household. I had underestimated the impact that hiring another head of household would have on me. I lay awake many nights trying to figure out what I would do if we failed. I knew Donna and her family would be fine. Mary Jo, the kids, and I could stay with my parents, but there certainly wasn't enough couch space at my parents' place for Alan's family too.

To be honest, that realization didn't hit me until he walked into the office for his first day of work. Obviously, looking back, I wouldn't have done anything differently; however, I didn't realize the impact that weight would have on me. In hindsight, that's likely a good thing, as I may have delayed making that first hire due to a fear that never became a reality.

Everything I Could Do vs Everything I Should Do

Hiring decisions were only a fraction of what consumed my time as I began to turn my vision into reality. In the first year of the business, I put any and all time into the company. Working 100-110 hours per week, seven days per week, I was doing everything from hiring to client meetings to preparing and sending out invoices and, of course, the engineering we were paid for. In hindsight, I know that was way too many hours, but at the time, I needed to know that I was doing everything I could to get the business off the ground. I also felt that I needed Mary Jo to know that I was doing everything that I could do.

The reality is that I didn't have to do everything I *could* do; I had to do everything that I *should* do. Everything I should do for the business would've likely taken 50–60 hours per week. Spending the other 50 or so hours with the family, being a good father and husband, and getting some rest and exercise would've likely been a much better use of my time. I've since learned the benefits of a well-rested, happy mindset.

I distinctly remember one Sunday when Mary Jo brought the kids to the office. Gavin was four, Adanya was two, and Julia was still in Mary Jo's arms. The kids were looking around the office with curiosity and amazement. Suddenly, Gavin turned and looked at me and said, "Is this where you live?" Wow, was that a punch in the gut. Most of the time, I got home well after the kids went to sleep. I'd go in, give them a kiss goodnight, and then leave again in the morning before they woke up, giving them another kiss while they slept. So it made sense that they didn't even realize I was there at night. I'd love to say that those words were what instantly transformed me into a 50–60-hour work week, but they weren't. They resonated for sure and likely caused me to dial it back sometimes, but unfortunately, nothing drastic. At least not for another few years until we had some more stability and predictability.

I just thank God that I eventually changed my ways. To be clear, I don't have anything against working longer hours when necessary. I take pride in being a hard worker, and I believe it's a great virtue. It's when I misused it as a badge of honor or simply to justify my efforts that I realized it was a mistake. Again, I didn't have to do everything I could for the business; I had to do everything I *should* do.

As I think back to the early days and about what really would have made me productive instead of working as many hours as I did, I feel that more time with Mary Jo, especially dates, the occasional overnight trip, and more one-to-one time with the kids would have been better.

And time present with the family in general would have recharged me in a way that I would have been more energized and more focused while actually in the office working. Additionally, if I had done something like Hal Elrod's *Miracle Morning*, or at least an abridged version of it, where I could do some exercise, journaling, prayer, reflection, and thinking about the big picture, it would have been incredibly valuable to me for my day. I should have spent time processing what I learned each and every week so that I would learn faster and more deeply.

How are you currently spending your time? Are you doing everything you *can* do or everything you *should* do?

Dear Brian,

Five months after you started the business, I remember the day you and I took Julia, our youngest at the time, into Lenox Hill Hospital. Julia was born with a hemangioma, a large birthmark on the tip of her nose that the amazing Dr. Weiner had been monitoring and, at the age of 10 months, had decided it was time to remove.

Although the procedure was small and she would be discharged the same day from the hospital, it was the first time you and I had experienced anything like this with any of the kids. The thought of Julia, our little peanut at the time, receiving anesthesia made us both extremely nervous. As we waited in the waiting room while Julia was undergoing her procedure, your phone rang.

You had placed a bid for a project; this project would have been a huge opportunity for the business. It would have been just the break we had been praying for. I watched your eyes intently as you spoke and quickly came to the realization you did not get the job. When you hung up, my heart sank for you. I could see the disappointment in your eyes. And I couldn't help but think, "Really, God, can't you see the fear and doubt creeping into him?" As I questioned why our Lord would allow this to happen, you bravely shrugged off your disappointment and said, "This is not what's important right now."

They called us back to the recovery room soon after your call ended, and there was Julia, waking up beautifully from her procedure. The doctors could not have been happier with the outcome of her procedure. As we drove home from Manhattan, neither one of us spoke about your call, and, in fact, it wasn't brought up again. I look back at your courage and your faith that day. There was no "What am I going to do now?" or "How could they have not chosen us for the project?" Your priority that day, as it is every day, was our Lord, myself, and the kids. It wasn't long after that day in Lenox Hill Hospital, maybe a week or two, that the business's phone certainly started to ring.

Our 20-year marriage is filled with countless examples, just like this one above. When I was questioning the Lord and venting my dismay at how he could allow this to happen to your attempts to start a company built on integrity and value, you were the rock; you were our strength. And the days when you felt doubt creeping in,

God gave me the nudge, reminding me to be strong, to be your rock for a change. I think of this day and what an absolute blessing it is to have a marriage built on faith. Adversity and doubt just really do not stand a chance.

I love you,
MJ

Landing the First Project

After months of roller-coaster ups and downs for what felt like great opportunities that didn't end up in signed contracts, we finally landed our first project. As our family's savings account dwindled steadily, the urgency to land work became very real, and so my fear of cold calling dissipated. It's funny how that happens.

After blindly reaching out to literally hundreds of potential clients to introduce myself, I spoke with a property manager who had a difficult building with very little money to spend. Perfect. They needed a leak investigation performed for minimal cost and as quickly as possible. Again, perfect. I was so hungry for work that none of those red flags mattered. I submitted a proposal for $2,000 for what should've been a $6,000 project; I just needed that first project.

Several days later, I received a call from the client stating that they wanted to award me the project, but could I do it for $350? Ughhh, really? Well, $350 that month would be better than the zeros I had been putting up over and over again. So, I accepted the reduced offer and received a signed contract. Although the contract was for a fraction of the real cost of the project, I had my first project. It felt fantastic. And yes, I still have a copy of that check framed.

In one of his first TED Talks, Simon Sinek describes the law of diffusion of innovation. Essentially, he very eloquently discusses the type of client that is willing to be the first. He refers to them as innovators versus those who are comfortable being the second client, who are referred to as early adopters and then the majority.[2] It's really a fascinating concept I wish I considered when deciding who to target. Instead of hundreds of phone calls with a shotgun-style approach, I may have used more of a sniper rifle approach to target the clients I thought would be in the first two groups.

Although this new client would not likely have otherwise been an innovator, their financial position and urgency forced them to be. Well, either way, I had my first client. I've learned that business development is like a snowball rolling downhill—really, all of business is. It takes a lot to get the first little snowball formed and rolling, but once it starts to roll, it builds size and momentum. That certainly was the case for us.

What feels like less than a few days after receiving the verbal approval for our first project, I was asked to meet a different potential client at a building. The owner was not happy with their current engineer and was looking to part ways amicably. They needed someone who could come in, pick up where the other engineer left off, and do it within the remaining budget. Now, this project had a much healthier budget than the first, even with part of it used up by the original engineer. We had a brief conversation about existing conditions. I must've given them confidence in my ability to do the project because they wanted me to start right away. I was pumped; the snowball was starting to roll.

I had been very honest with the client and shared that my business was relatively new. The property manager was also a new firm, so clearly, I had either an innovator or an early adopter. As I started to walk away, they called out and said, "Oh, we forgot to ask: What other projects are you working on?" I enthusiastically responded, "I'm working on a leak investigation downtown for a–." They cut me off. "Good enough. We just want to make sure you have something else." So, they were an early adopter, which makes sense. They were an established building but needed to be conscious of budget and weren't in the most attractive geographic area.

That project was a tremendous success, resulting in several more opportunities in that building alone and over 100 more with that property manager over the next decade. As it turns out, the discount I gave on the first project was likely the best marketing money I ever spent. As a friend of mine recently said, "Everybody wants to be the second client." Landing that first project was crucial.

The Joy of the Check Run

The excitement of having the first job under your belt is only matched by the thrill of getting paid for that first job. You've presumably set up your business bank account, but with a check in hand, what now?

I heard about the concept of the "joy of the check run" while amongst a group of entrepreneurs. As soon as we heard the phrase, we started to smile. The check run is when you receive a check and run to the bank—pretty self-explanatory. The magnitude, though, especially as a new small business, is massive. Whether the check came via mail or was handed to me, I needed to get it to the bank as quickly as possible, so off I ran, literally.

There are some trying moments from the early days that I look back on that still give me stress, and there are others that make me smile. The joy of the check run is definitely one that makes me smile. I still get excited when checks come into the office; that exhilarating feeling never goes away. It's a great feeling knowing that a client is satisfied with you, happy with your services, and willing to pay for them.

Some of our clients were challenging to get paid from, but some of them were really, really fantastic and understood that we were a very small business and cash was critical to our success.

In the early days, one of our largest clients—which, at one point, was 85 percent of our revenue—had a CFO who was such a nice guy and completely understood the importance attached to our business. He would call me and tell me that he had the check processed for an invoice that we had sent, often less than a week earlier. "The check is ready. Do you want me to put it in the mail, or will you pick it up?" He always knew the answer was that I would pick it up.

I would tell him that I was on site and would be there in about thirty-five minutes. Inevitably, he would chuckle because he knew the drive from my office in New Jersey to his office in the Bronx was thirty-five minutes. If I wanted to walk from the site to his office, that would take about three minutes.

He called because he knew how important those checks were to the business. I gladly drove across the George Washington Bridge, paid the tolls, picked up the check, and drove directly to the bank, knowing their checks were going to cover costs for a while,

Clients like that are truly, truly valuable—for startups and, really, for all businesses. When you find clients like that, do everything you can to keep them.

Prior to starting the business, I was like most non-business owners and didn't realize that the owner was often the last to get paid if they got paid at all. I'm not saying this was a good strategy, and I definitely wouldn't recommend it, but it was probably four years before I actually went on the payroll and received a regular income. At that point, we had ten employees.

So, what makes the joy of the check run that much sweeter is that we, as business owners, often do it more for our team than we do for ourselves.

The Newsletter

The team was growing, as was our client list, but as an entrepreneur, I was constantly considering how to make our business better. One of our best early returns on an investment was our email newsletter. When we started the business in 2010, email spam wasn't nearly the issue it is today. So, it was easier for our emails to make it through to our readers than it would be now. For a relatively minimal subscription cost, we created a template and a mailing list and were up and running.

At the start, our mailing list had a disproportionate number of Sullivans as it was made up of more friends and family than potential clients. However, we also included contractors and other industry colleagues that we thought might find the content interesting and beneficial. We felt the purpose was to remind people that we existed and stay top of mind, not to try to directly sell. So, we had technical content that we felt was informative and educational, not sales-y. We also included items completely unrelated to our area of expertise: a quote of the month and monthly recommendations for restaurants, books, and apps.

Just like the business, the newsletter was a snowball that had to start rolling. We didn't get much feedback in the first few months other than from family and friends, which is a great reason to have them on the list. However, after a few months, we started to notice that our name recognition picked up significantly. As I would be introduced to people at events, I began to hear comments like, "Oh, yeah, I know you guys, so and so forwarded me your newsletter. I didn't realize you were that large already." There were two of us on the team, and one of those two was part-time, yet the newsletter made us seem "large." It also allowed us to differentiate ourselves to a wider audience as a professional, trustworthy firm that wanted to provide value first.

Initially, I would write the 2–3 technical articles, and Donna and I would share the responsibilities of the monthly recommendations; however, as we increased our team size, we started to spread the responsibility out, and each team member was required to contribute. Although some saw this responsibility as a burden, most embraced it as a way to enhance their individual professional brand and recognition. The one constant that remained was that Donna, the former teacher, always reviewed the content to ensure it was grammatically correct and an enjoyable read.

The direct sales that came from the newsletter were not very quantifiable, or at least we didn't measure the ROI, but the increased name recognition and frequent conversations that we had with clients, industry professionals, and contractors about items in the newsletter were justification alone for the time and effort. Eventually, we did have friends and family make introductions that led to work that I don't believe would've occurred from conversations over drinks alone. The final and possibly largest justification came from a seemingly random phone call from a relatively new property manager tasked with finding the right help to address a persistent issue her building was experiencing. As she searched the internet for her issue, she came across an article I had written for our newsletter that was posted in our blog.

As it turned out, she worked on a good-sized campus in NY for a very large client who would provide a significant amount of future work, becoming our second-highest client by revenue and eventually being the catalyst for the launch of our Boston office.

What's your version of the newsletter?
What are the low-cost, high-value methods that you can use to differentiate your new business from the competition?

Supporting Players

No successful business is sustained without people behind the scenes supporting the efforts. Think about when you bring a newborn child home and the support the caregivers need to survive the first few weeks and months. Friends and neighbors bring meals so the physically exhausted new parents can nourish their bodies. Family members come to visit and allow the parents to attempt to get a few hours of much-needed sleep. The support of people around the new parents is paramount to feeling "successful" in the early days.

As with the early days with a newborn, no great business venture can be accomplished without the support of the people behind the scenes. I was fortunate to not only have my parents' blessing but, maybe more importantly, Mary Jo's.

A few months after starting the business, I was stressed and focused on my own workload, struggles, etc., but I took the opportunity to attend a networking event. There, I struck up a conversation with an engineer who was near the end of his career. He had many typical questions about the business and my family, but he seemed most curious about Mary Jo's support.

After chatting for five minutes or so, he said, "You're so lucky that your wife is supportive of your dream." I smiled because it was something I was subconsciously grateful for. The man's expression darkened as he continued. "I always wanted to start my own firm," he admitted, "but my wife wouldn't let me. I've always resented her because of that."

Wow! His words silenced the sounds in the crowded, noisy bar and hit me profoundly. He was right; I was incredibly fortunate to have a supportive spouse. At that point, though, I had no idea how fortunate I was.

Dear Brian,

You were about eight months into your entrepreneurial journey, and the Moody's had invited us and the Conlon's over for dinner and drinks. We were super excited, not only for what would probably be our first night out without the kids since you started the business but also because we would be hanging out with two of our favorite couples. It had been a slow go for the company, to put it mildly, up until this point, but nothing both of us weren't prepared for or expecting, so we hoped. Although we expected things to start slowly for the business, it didn't necessarily mean we weren't hoping it would just take off.

You and I were never ones to bicker with each other, but I could feel our impatience with one another beginning to creep up. We were starting to get upset with each other over the smallest of things, and both of us just seemed to be overly sensitive. I knew seeing Pat and Moody would be a great boost for you, as well as a much-needed night out for the two of us.

The girls and I were laughing and having our side conversation in the same room as you three boys. I could overhear one of the guys asking you, "How's work? How's the business going so far?" And your response, I remember as clear as day, was, "You mean my new hobby? It's going great. Not sure you can call it a business." The three of you chuckled, but my heart sank when I heard your words. It was certainly not unlike you to take a jab at yourself, especially to make others laugh, but this comment was more than that. You showed your vulnerability like you were beginning to doubt you could do this, a characteristic you rarely display.

As the girls continued talking, I just felt sad inside, thinking of how the last few weeks had been going for us. I was drawn back into the girls' conversation when Jen asked me if I had ever heard of Proverbs 31. When I replied no, she said, "You would love it," and quickly helped me sign up on my phone to receive their daily spiritual reflection e-mail. It's funny how God works; the first e-mail popped up on my phone, and I stood in Allison's kitchen reading it. It was a dialogue between a woman who was struggling with her husband and their marriage as of late and one of her friends from her Bible study class.

> *The friend told her after listening to her vent her dismay with her marriage, "Honey, you've gotta decide if you're gonna spend your energy fighting with your husband or fighting for him." She continued, "Every wife was made to be a warrior. Take . . . the sword of the Spirit, which is the word of God. Pray always. Pray in the Spirit. Pray about everything in every way you know how!" (Ephesians 6:17b-18 [The Voice]).*
>
> *I devoured those words of insight as if God was whispering to me. That night during our ride home, I could not have been more grateful for that evening. God put us exactly where we needed to be. I was ready to go to battle for you and your vision. I believed in you from the start, so why would I choose the hardest point of your entrepreneurial journey to get weak on you? That wasn't me, and that's not us. God is so good!*
>
> *I love you,*
> *MJ*

As the African proverb goes, "It takes a village to raise a child," well, the same can be said for starting a business. We had our families, our friends, mentors, and others lifting us up.

Who is in your village?
Don't be afraid or embarrassed to seek support from your village.
Use your village for inspiration and perspective too.

Dr. Hourani

Entrepreneurs find inspiration from many people and places. Inspiration feeds the passion that creates the desire to pursue a venture. Where that inspiration comes from is often an inspiring story in itself.

As an undergraduate student at Manhattan College, I had the distinct pleasure of learning from Dr. Moujalli Hourani, one of the most remarkable human beings I've ever met. To be very clear, he was not one of my favorite professors because he was an easy A; in fact, he was the opposite. He was a very difficult C, at least for me anyway. The man is brilliant and incredibly driven, and he expected the same level of drive from all of his students. He was one of my favorite teachers of all time because of his faith, dedication, and focus on getting the best from all of his students.

What I didn't recognize initially, though, was that he did not view me as a disappointment because I didn't get straight A's. He appreciated my strong faith and involvement in other activities and apparently saw some leadership traits inside of me that I didn't fully recognize. In my junior year, he encouraged me to run for president of the school's Civil Engineering Society, which may not seem like a big deal, but for me, it truly was. That role led to my involvement in the governance of the school of engineering and, eventually, becoming an officer for the entire student body. Not something I would've at all thought was possible without a friendly nudge from Dr. Hourani. This passion for leadership was my first glimpse of how I could differentiate myself from other engineers.

I would imagine that he likely knew that I didn't work as hard as I should've on my school work, and I'm sure that disappointed him; regardless, he didn't cast me aside. In fact, at one point, I approached him as he was the head of the department, and I wanted to set myself up for a really easy semester in my senior year. I only needed 12 credits to graduate, but I needed his permission to take less than the 15 credits included with tuition. He proceeded to have a long and very loving conversation with me about why I should get the maximum return on the investment that my parents and I were paying for. It would've been very easy for him to have simply granted the permission and rushed me out of his office, but that's not who he is.

As I wrapped up my college career, I received a civil engineering award and was thrilled that Dr. Hourani was there to celebrate with my parents; after all, he was one of the reasons that I was receiving the award. Several years after graduation, when I was considering going to graduate school, I reconnected with Dr Hourani. I popped by his office, and he didn't skip a beat. He immediately welcomed me into his office, and we caught up personally. Then, he gave me very straightforward, honest guidance on why I should go to Manhattan College for my graduate degree. So I did.

While in graduate school, I stayed in contact with this great man and started to grow in friendship. So, when I started the business, he was a natural mentor, sharing his sage advice and wisdom. He turned out to be one of our strongest cheerleaders and even helped us with our hiring needs by connecting us with graduating engineers who he thought would be a great fit for the type of work we do and, more importantly, the type of values-based culture we created.

I now have the pleasure of considering Dr. Hourani a personal friend and mentor, both professionally and personally. I pray that he writes a book one day soon to share his personal story. His devotion to our Lord, his devotion to his wife and family, and his devotion to his students have had a transformational impact on so many.

Who is your Dr. Hourani?
Who is that individual who motivates you to be a better person while simultaneously believing in you and pushing you to accomplish more in all aspects of life?

Peter Sweeney

As a graduate student at Manhattan College, I had the pleasure of taking several classes taught by Peter Sweeney. Peter had a very successful professional career as an engineer and was subsequently teaching as an adjunct professor to help impart his wisdom and experience to young professionals.

Despite his very successful career, Peter has a very humble personality that makes him very approachable. So, I frequently connected with him during graduate school and sought his advice. After completing my graduate degree and eventually starting the business, I reached out to him again, connecting over coffee so I could gain some insight. Peter was a huge help with the guidance that he provided, but even more so in a surprising way shortly afterward. He was working with a group of fellow alumni to save the Catholic elementary school in Manhattan that he attended as a child. The group was starting a fundraising campaign to address much-needed repairs to the school. Before they could do that, they needed an assessment of the exterior of the building performed by an engineer to determine how much work was required and the cost of those repairs. Peter knew that was my specialty, so he reached out to see if I had the time and interest. Since the business was still getting off the ground and revenue was very low, I had a lot of both.

I have a deep affection for Catholic schools, so I was eager to lend a hand. Despite Peter's protests, I insisted on performing my service for the investigation and report for free. After all, I wasn't doing much valuable with my time, and the money they saved could be put toward the repairs.

I provided the report to Peter and hoped that they would be able to raise the funds to do the repairs for the benefit of the school. However, I also hoped that I would have a chance to be involved in the larger project. At the same time, though, I knew that the larger project would be run by the Archdiocese of New York, and like many large potential clients, they had their preferred vendors.

After a few months passed, Peter reached out again to let me know they raised the funds and would like to move forward with the project, but just as I thought, the Archdiocese would be handling the project. Despite his own focus on trying to get the project approved, Peter took the time to put in a strong word for me. I was on the list to be considered and eventually was awarded the project.

The school was the first project we performed for the Archdiocese of New York, but certainly not the last. It ended up being a springboard for us to develop a strong relationship with the Archdiocese, where we performed around a hundred projects over the years. Through those relationships formed with personnel and other organizations involved in those projects, we landed work with several other large clients.

Of course, for all that to play out, we had to perform well on the projects, but we would never have had the chance to perform if Peter hadn't given us the initial opportunity and then went to bat for us with the Archdiocese. Oftentimes, people will not take the extra step to go to bat for someone and put their neck on the line as they have their own priorities that they don't want to see derailed. Peter reinforced for me the importance of taking the time to have someone's back and put my neck on the line for those I believe deserve it.

Who is your Peter Sweeney?

Who is the professional you have on such a high pedestal that you're nervous about reaching out to but are willing and eager to help if you just ask?

On a side note, it's interesting to me to see how many very successful people are willing to sacrifice their time to meet with younger professionals if they are willing to ask.

Dan Connolly

As I launched the business, I reached out to a friend of mine from college who had started his own engineering firm several years earlier. Dan Connolly is a great engineer, husband, and dad and has a strong faith in God, so his words of wisdom mean a great deal to me. Dan had been through the weeds and was a very calming voice. He also has a great sense of humor that was often needed.

When I started the business, since I was a NJ-based engineering firm performing work in NY, I needed several different NY personal and business licenses. The process seemed straightforward enough, and I had started it several months before launching the business, which seemed responsible enough. However, due to some errors and general bureaucratic inefficiencies, my application was held up for many months. As the stress caused by this would hit in certain peaks, I would share my frustration with Dan, and he would say some wise-ass comment to make me laugh and then give solid advice.

I remember one call where I was panicking, and Dan pointed out, "Well, the good news is you don't have any work anyway, so it's not an issue." It was a funny reality that made me laugh, but then he followed up with, "And when you do land work, which you will, you have options available to perform the work legally anyway." I had sought advice from attorneys and other business owners and had solutions in place if necessary. Dan knew that, but as my stress increased, those weren't top of mind for me.

Dan was always great with what I call the Optimistic Truth. He very easily could've said, "Why would you have started a business without having the proper licenses in place for the market you want to serve? That's irresponsible." That would be true, but it would've been the Pessimistic Truth, which would not have helped me in that situation. He also did not provide false assurance that would've set me up for future failure. Instead, he shared the Optimistic Truth, the actual reality viewed from a positive mindset.

Conversely, I got the pessimistic truth when I shared the news of starting my business with a friend of mine who knew me well professionally and had started his own business six months earlier. I enthusiastically shared the news with him that I turned in my resignation and was going to start my own firm. He asked if I could meet him that same day, so I did. The first thing he said to me was I had made a terrible mistake; I should withdraw my resignation and stay where I was.

Alright, so it's not at all the reaction I was hoping for or needed. Taking this step to submit my resignation and let the world know that I was starting my own business was incredibly nerve-wracking and created a lot of self-doubt; this certainly didn't help.

It wasn't until years later, when we were talking about the early days of our businesses, that I realized that my friend was warning me because he was going through struggles in starting his business and, as a friend, was trying to help me avoid those struggles. He was likely talking to himself, not to me. However, I took it as him not having confidence in me as an individual when it was his lack of confidence in himself.

I've since realized that it's important to know why someone might be showing concern or providing negative feedback.

Who is your Dan Connolly?

Who is your trusted peer who has already walked the road you're walking and has a positive but realistic view of what lies ahead? Who will tell you the Optimistic Truth and make you laugh when you need it?

Dear Brian,

Just the other day we were reminiscing about our journey throughout the last fourteen years, soon after you started the business, and Gavin happened to be in your office at the time we were talking. You said you felt guilty for sometimes coming home and venting your frustrations about your day or the business with me.

You said if you were to give advice to future business owners, it would be to remain sensitive to doing this to your spouse or significant other.

You said to me, "Hearing me vent about my day was probably the last thing you needed or wanted to hear when I walked in the door late at night." I quickly responded, "Absolutely not! Having you talk to me and share with me your day—the good as well as the frustrating parts—made me feel part of your day. It was somewhat of a filler for all the hours we were spending apart. The days and weeks apart from each other were long for us, but when you came home and opened up about your day, it brought us together.

I recognized early on that you weren't seeking my sound advice on how to operate the business; you were looking for a sounding board, a confidant. I didn't have to be intimidated by how my degree in nursing lacked entrepreneurial disciplines such as finance and management. I could listen to you and reiterate back to you what you were telling me. I could ask you questions and interpret a situation through my eyes and my heart after hearing what you explained to me. These conversations not only gave us much-needed time together, but they made me feel valued, like, in some way, I was part of your growing company. And, in fact, as these conversations continued for the past fourteen years, I began to appreciate all I learned from you.

Hearing your phone conversations when you were working from home or listening to your stories and how you interacted with people proved to be so valuable for me and for us as a couple. I think a huge reward that came from all of these interactions was seeing how beneficial it could be to incorporate some of your exceptional leadership and entrepreneurial skills into our marriage and family life.

I love you,
MJ

Hey Mary Jo,

The older I get, the more wisdom I recognize in seeking the counsel of others. Lord knows the stories in this book are a small fraction of the impact that others have had on my decisions. Whether it was you, family, friends, or advisers, I have grown less and less reluctant to seek advice.

Truthfully, though, I never should've been reluctant. After all, Jesus sought the counsel of his apostles, the Pope seeks the counsel of his cardinals, and our good friend Bishop Kevin Sweeney relies on the strength of his diocesan priests. If these great men can ask for help, then who am I to resist it?

In addition to seeking the wisdom of each other, though, the importance of prayer can't be understated. In 2014, Pope Francis described prayer as a way to seek the counsel of God. Through prayer, we can hear the Holy Spirit guide us. He went on to say, "The gift of counsel, like all spiritual gifts, needs to be cultivated through prayer, by which we become attuned to the voice of the Spirit and conformed to the heart of Christ."

Counsel really is a gift, and like all great gifts, it benefits the giver just as much as the receiver, so we should seek it as much as possible and be willing to give counsel to those who seek it.

Love,
Brian

III

TODDLER YEARS

Train children in the right way, and when old, they will not stray.

—Proverbs 22:6

When raising children, the toddler years are full of exciting "firsts:" first words, first steps, first tooth, first real foods. . . . It's a time when parents feel some relief knowing their child survived the first year. But countering these thrilling first events is the terrifying realization of the new dangers for the child and trials for the parents. Providing children with the independence they need to learn to walk and eventually run, knowing that this means they will fall down, is pivotal growth for the child and the parent.

Similarly, as owners, if we are to allow the business to grow, we must provide independence to our team and let them run fast and fall down. We can be there to provide encouragement, show them how to get back up, and occasionally temper the fall, but we must let them fall.

Not So Successful Early Hires

As I write this book, it feels like we knocked it out of the park with all of our early hires. However, that's definitely not the case. Since I handled almost the entire interview process back then, whenever we had a miss hire, it was easy to look back at some glaring red flags that I justified to myself or just ignored and didn't trust my gut.

One such team member was a young man who had been out of work for close to one year since graduating with an engineering degree. This was during a time when there was a shortage of engineers and ample opportunities. It was hard not to have a job back then. During the interview, he didn't clearly answer what he had been doing for the year. I dismissed that and other issues because he seemed like a nice guy. Well, he was a nice guy, but as you likely figured out already, he wasn't very driven, was late for work regularly, was slow to get his work done, and didn't have the autonomy that we needed. For the love of God, I couldn't even get the kid to wear a belt to work.

Another classic case was a woman near the end of her career who needed a second chance. I was happy to give her that second chance until I realized that on her resume and during the interview, she had greatly exaggerated, if not flat-out lied about her skills. She did not have the basic skills to perform the role. For example, for several weeks, she simply answered the phone by saying "Hello" instead of our typical professional greeting that we went over with her every day. Each morning when she arrived, we had to show her how to turn on her computer. Those are just two of the many, many items that clearly pointed out she didn't have any of the basic skills needed for the role. Obviously, we had to let her go, the lack of basic skills was something we might have been able to overcome, but the broken trust and blatant lying on her resume was a deal breaker. One of the ripple effects of her fabricated resume was that we actually started talking about giving basic computer proficiency tests to admins moving forward, which would've been counter to the culture we were trying really hard to establish.

There was also a guy who joined and was unmanageable, arrogant, and combative from day one. Although we were being very fair with our performance expectations and giving him ample feedback and opportunities to respond to that feedback, his behavior became more and more concerning. After what felt like two very long weeks, he quit. We later learned that he had actually just taken two weeks' vacation from his previous job and decided to come over and try working for an engineering firm to see if he would like it. Well, he didn't, and neither did we.

The common threads of the three examples above were that they were all referred to us by people who didn't know us that well—they were friends of friends. I took the referral as justification for not performing a reference check with proper due diligence, and I didn't really ask a lot of probing questions. I just assumed they'd be a great fit. Most of our hiring success came from referrals by friends who know and understand me well, as well as the type of culture we were trying to build.

Successful Early Hires

In 2012, we hired roughly eight people. Five of those turned out to be absolute rockstars who stayed with us long-term. I guess there's something about the type of person who's drawn to a scrappy startup, where conversations are focused on what can be rather than what has been.

At the start of 2012, we still had our two-room office with four employees working in it. The office consisted of two desks with desk chairs and two folding tables with folding chairs. Recognizing that this could appear ridiculous and was not a great look for recruiting, minutes before Mike walked in the door for his interview, we quickly moved the folding tables and everything else that didn't look professional into an unlocked, empty office down the hall. Looking back now, I'm not sure if this improved the look of our office or seemed absurd that we had four people working in an office with just two desks. To be fair, it wasn't a total bait and switch because, by the time Mike would start, we planned to have a new, larger office with proper furniture.

Mike was a great early hire, as he shared my scrappy mindset, was a jack of all trades, and had a great ability to roll with it—all skills that were critical to our early success. As we grew, we were able to bring in people who were more specialized in their skill sets. But early on, we needed our team to be able to wear many different hats. Mike certainly wore many hats throughout his tenure, which helped free me up to continue to grow the business and chase new opportunities. One that he really excelled at was recruiting. Mike handled all of the initial outreach, communication, and first interviews with candidates. His passion for our team and what we were accomplishing resonated deeply with them. By the time they made it to my third and final interview, they were so energized and optimistic about joining the team that we very rarely had someone say no to an offer, which allowed us to be incredibly selective.

The first engineering college graduate we recruited was Kevin. It was April when we learned that we needed to hire quickly. And we wanted a recent college graduate to help us grow to the next level of team members. From day one, it was clear that Kevin was wise beyond his years. The only reason that he was still available just several weeks before graduation was because he was taking six weeks after graduation to travel around Europe, and no employer wanted to wait for him to return. I liked Kevin right out of the gate, but what sealed it for me was when I sent him an email to his college email address and received an out-of-office response. I knew he was special—it was rare to see a college student with such a professional, forward-thinking mindset. Kevin eventually grew into our VP of Operations and was a pivotal team member and friend.

We often look back and laugh at the fact that one of the first things I noticed was the out-of-office message. I think about how short-sighted other employers were and that they wouldn't wait six weeks for this rockstar who stayed with our team for 13 years. It was hard when I was in the moment and really needed somebody, but having my eye on the long term always paid off tremendously, even in the short term.

As I think back to our first successful hires, specifically to Kevin, if I were starting the firm again and looking for new employees, some of Kevin's greatest strengths are exactly what I would look for. Kevin had a great ability to roll with it. His training was not very formal or intentional at all; it was more baptism by fire. I just brought him out to the field, showed him a few things, and then sent him on his way.

I can't pretend like I fully recognized it in the interview process, but Kevin's out-of-office signature and his willingness to take six weeks to backpack around Europe were two important signs that he would be an independent, motivated, high achiever—exactly the skill set that we needed at the time.

Dear Brian,

I was folding laundry in the mud room, listening to a recording of Fr. Mike Schmitz on my Hallow app preach about the Gospel that past Sunday. His sermon brought me back to our upbringings and our four amazing parents, and to you, your faith in our Lord, and the courage it took for you to leave all the securities of a well-established engineering firm and go out and start your own. The Gospel that particular Sunday was John 3:16-18:

> *"God so loved the world that he gave his only son so that everyone that believes in Him might not perish but might have eternal life. For God did not send his son into the world to condemn the world, but that the world might be saved through him."*

After reading the Gospel and diving into God's message, Fr. Mike shared a story that a fellow priest friend had shared with him about his childhood. Fr. Mike's friend shared that when he and his brothers were young, their father had sat them down for the "priorities" talk. Their father stated that in his life, God was number 1, their mother was number 2, and they, his sons, were number 3. I remember that day finding that talk so profound between a father and his children. I thought back to my childhood and my parents as well as your parents. Now, neither you nor I had ever been given the "priorities" talk from our parents, but we knew this to be very true in our households just by witnessing our parents. While my father was not a practicing Catholic at all, if alive today and given the chance to ask him who was my Mom's top priority, there is no doubt he would tell me God and gracefully take the number two spot.

I thought not only how blessed you and I were to witness this in our parents but how this became true in our own marriage and our house as well. By being witnesses to our parents, we came into our marriage with clear-cut priorities: God is number 1, and we were each other's number 2's. I contemplated throughout the last 20 years about how we had stayed true to our priorities and how that gave us so much strength in our marriage. How living out those priorities allowed us to place emphasis where it was needed: God, each other, our family, and our community. Looking back, I could also see how having those priorities in place made starting a business, I wouldn't say, easier, but with a lot more ease. The success or failure of the business was somewhat irrelevant, if I can say that. Giving the business the freedom to fail, knowing that our priorities would be unscathed regardless of the outcome of the business, I truly believe, was a huge contributing factor to the company's success. No one's happiness or love was dependent on the success of the business. We both knew who number 1 was, and I thought what a gift having a foundation like this laid for you and me by our parents. What a gift of freedom to be given to a couple. This gift allowed me to be okay with my imperfections and shortcomings as your wife because your number 1 is perfect all the time. And where my insight, strength, and sometimes even love is lacking, God's is ever present for you. Our Lord always has your back when I come up short, what a gift to know that in our marriage!!!

I love you,
MJ

Networking and Peer Advisory Groups

I've always seen the benefit of having a solid network and peers to bounce ideas off of. However, when I started my business, my network of peers and fellow business owners was not as strong as I needed it to be. So, I decided to join a local networking group in my hometown, which was a nice, friendly group of people; however, they weren't connected to my target clients. Most of the group serviced my hometown in New Jersey while I was attempting to service New York City.

One of the huge benefits of the group, though, was the friendly nature that allowed me to get more comfortable with the concept of networking. I was able to continue to practice honing my introduction and my elevator pitch to a group of qualified professionals. I didn't land any new leads from the group, but I benefited tremendously from the practice of networking.

A friend of mine recently asked about the benefits of the networking groups I joined when I started the business. Essentially, I said, "Don't be too picky. If you find a group that isn't exactly what you're looking for, go anyway, get your reps in; it's great practice." Of course, we want to be in groups that allow us to benefit from their network and, similarly, allow the people in the group to benefit from our network. However, it does take a little practice to get to that point of being mutually beneficial. You want to be well prepared, so when you have the opportunity to be in a room or even invited to join a group, the interaction is as powerful and natural as you want it to be.

As for peer groups, I similarly saw the benefit of having other business owners to collaborate with, ask questions, share thoughts, and hear their feedback. The first peer group I joined was a forum-type group, where we met one Friday a month for about five hours. It was a good group to be a part of for the early days of the business because it didn't require a massive commitment, and I didn't have a lot of time or a lot of money to put towards it. Several of the members were really good-hearted business owners who cared deeply about the success of everyone in the group and were willing to share their lessons learned to help others avoid the same mistakes.

One of the best pieces of advice that I got from this group came from Jim, the gentleman who ran the group. I first met him at that networking group mentioned above. I was thinking of setting up a board of advisors, and I talked with him about it. He pointed out that the professionals that I could and would draw to a Board would be close family and friends, and they would be loyal to me to a fault and likely not give me the feedback that I need. Thankfully, he pointed me toward the forum group instead.

Even though I learned a lot from these groups, I eventually moved away from them and got involved with other networking groups that made more sense for my target client and other peer groups whose business owners had similar growth goals to mine. At one point, my friend Ross invited me to a meeting of the Executives Association of New York City. This is a group of business owners and executives who primarily service the New York City market. Just by the name alone, you can tell it was better suited for my target clients and where I was trying to grow the company. I'd like to pretend that after my first meeting, I saw the value in the group and decided to join. While I did see the value in the group, for some reason, I couldn't get over the hurdle that I belonged in the room and that I could justify the expense of the group.

Eventually, thanks to Ross's persistence, I got beyond the imposter syndrome and joined, and that group changed my trajectory. The business owners and executives in that group were like-minded, phenomenally smart businesspeople from all different industries. They all genuinely cared about the well-being and success of their teams, everyone in the group, and our families. By seeing the growth and accomplishments of many people in that room, I myself was further driven to continue to set higher goals and accomplish bigger feats.

The group was meant to be a networking group, but it was so much more. I became great friends with many of my fellow business owners. We shared many challenges within our businesses, but also challenges we faced at home, in our families, and in our faith. I'm very fortunate to still be great friends with many of those people today. It's been my experience that the right group is well worth the time and the money. And, in some instances, the more the time commitment, the better. The more time I put in, the more I got out.

I've learned that the keys to truly productive networking, like so much else in life, are intentionality and authenticity. The more intentional I was about who I wanted to meet and why, the more successful I was. One of the most intentional networkers that I know is Joe Apfelbaum. Joe is the CEO of Ajax Union and evyAI, as well as a LinkedIn expert and author. He is always willing to give his time and share his great tips. He even created a Checklist for Business Networking Success, which he discusses in his book, *High Energy Networking*. Also, the best networkers I know are incredibly authentic; they do what they say they will do; they are givers, not takers, and they genuinely care about the success of those with whom they develop relationships.

Who is your Ross?
Who in your circle is a great networker and is willing to invite you into their circle?

Recommended Reading List

I wasn't an avid reader until my mid-twenties when I learned the joys of reading for fun, which eventually led to reading personal and professional development books. The impact that the books I read had on me was incredibly valuable, so we decided to have a recommended reading list in the office. To further support the list and emphasize the value of reading, we made all books on the list free to our team members. They could take any book they wanted, whenever they wanted, as long as they committed to reading it. We also asked for suggestions for the recommended reading list so that we could continue to grow the list. As a result, the initial list of around 20 books grew to over 100. Appendix D, at the back of this book, has three of our recommended reading lists: one for books on business, one for books on families, and one for faith.

The presence of this list and the conversations that resulted were insightful in so many ways. We included a question on our performance reviews to determine how many books people read each year and how many of those were from the list. It was not surprising at all that the people who read the most books from the list were also the ones growing the most personally and professionally. It was similarly curious to me how people would wonder why they weren't advancing as professionals, yet they weren't doing something as simple as reading books provided for free. We had some people on our team who would read two fiction books per month but wouldn't read a single development book in a year. We also had team members who wanted to be paid for the time spent reading, and another shared that he didn't read books on our list but found others similar to them and read those instead. It rarely surprised me to see an employee who didn't put in minimal effort to read the free books leave the company. Perhaps one day, those people will see the value we provided with those free personal development books.

Reading was such a big part of how we were trying to grow our team as individuals that to celebrate our 5th anniversary as a company, we sent all of our clients a copy of *The Daily Drucker* as a small token of appreciation. *The Daily Drucker* is a culmination of the great Peter Drucker's thoughts and quotes distilled into daily bites. It was really well received by many of our clients as a unique token of appreciation, different from the standard water bottle or mug with a company logo on it. Of course, there was a branding component to our effort. We had our logo embossed on the front of the book so that each time the client looked at the book, they'd remember us. We have provided similar gifts on subsequent anniversaries and still have clients casually bring up the books in conversations.

How frequently are you reading or listening to books and content that will help you along your path? How much of that time is devoted to business? Family? Faith?

Delivering Feedback

As Henry Ford famously said, "The only thing worse than training your employees and having them leave is not training them and having them stay." We carried this mindset into our philosophy for performance reviews and feedback. As a result, we often had some difficult conversations, but in our opinion, that's what good leaders do.

I've often had discussions with leaders on our team about the difference between being nice and being weak. This typically came in advance of difficult conversations that they were preparing for with their team members. In a performance review or, it's much easier for a leader to be "nice" and simply provide only positive feedback, even if it's not deserved. It's my experience that they are not being nice at all but rather weak. If we as leaders see any area that a team member needs to improve, we need to share that with them in order to help them advance their career, make more money, create new opportunities, etc. If we don't share this feedback with them, we are setting them up for failure and potentially having to be fired. From this perspective, it's clear to see which one is really the nice path.

We never want to be a capital "J" Jerk but rather a small "j" jerk, as identified in Patrick Lencioni's article, "The jerk Factor." A small "j" jerk refers "to someone who is willing to say or do something that pushes a peer or subordinate far out of their comfort zone in order to make them or the team better." While a capital "J" Jerk refers to "the ones who consistently demonstrate harshness and attitude, with no apparent reason."[3] Small "j" jerks are great people who have our best interests at heart, even if we don't see it in the moment. They are critical to the success and growth of organizations and the individuals inside them.

On his *At the Table* podcast, Patrick recently hosted Craig Groeschel, Pastor and Founder of Life Church, and they discussed this topic further. Craig had some great insight into why churches need to avoid being weak with their team. If churches can be compassionate, mission-driven, and avoid being weak, then we certainly can too. The entire discussion is a fantastic summary of great organizational leadership and well worth the listen.[4]

When delivered in the right setting with the right tone and context, feedback can be truly transformational. I had a discussion with one young professional on our team who was living with her parents at home after college to save money. However, the reality was that her parents' well-intentioned support was impacting how she was perceived by her team members, as well as her ability to stay at the office a little late and even attend industry events. In order to continue growing personally and professionally, she needed to set some good guidelines with her parents or move out. To her credit, she received the feedback well and acted on it, and the impact resulted in immediate maturation, personally and professionally.

Can you be the small "j" jerk that your business and your team need?

Learning Moments

Just like a child, new businesses experience growing pains, usually evolving from mistakes being made. I've always learned the best from my own experiences, especially my mistakes. In my business, I wanted to foster an environment where team members could share their mistakes and get help solving them rather than try to hide or cover them up. We all know that if we try to hide or learn from our mistakes, they will likely only compound or get worse. Additionally, if we hide them, we don't learn from them, so to embrace the mindset we wanted, we called our mistakes "learning moments."

When I read Dave Ramsey's philosophy on sharing learning moments with the team, it gave me the courage to share my own and ask our team members to be vulnerable and share theirs as well. The concept can be a tough one for new team members to be comfortable with. So, I had to lead by example and make sure I was sharing more mistakes than anyone else. This took a lot of courage, vulnerability, and a lot of learning moments. Fortunately, I make a ton of mistakes, so coming up with material to share was never a problem.

We asked our team to share learning moments publicly with the whole team and, most importantly, what they learned from them and how they would handle the situation differently in the future. The mindset behind this was when I make a mistake and have to suffer through resolving that mistake, why should I not share that experience with the team that I love to help them avoid making the same mistake? To be clear, mistakes made out of laziness or carelessness were not tolerated, nor were they repeated mistakes. However, mistakes made out of reaching outside of our comfort zones or trying something new are how rapid growth happens.

Based on this exercise, we decided to have an annual "Best Mistake Award." To be clear, this was not to reward the biggest mistake but rather to have some fun and laugh at ourselves, acknowledging that some of the mistakes we made are very, very funny. Every year at our annual retreat, we would nominate three or four of the funniest learning moments of the past year. The nominees would retell their stories, and then we would all vote. The winner would receive a giant eraser and have their name placed on a plaque in the office. We had a lot of good-natured laughs as a result. In hindsight, it's no surprise that it was the team members who grew the most that were repeat nominees.

Some of my favorite, not the funniest, learning moment stories had a financial impact. I guess, really, they always do. In the very early days, I made a mistake with our largest client. I accidentally identified mortar that had been applied on the wrong floor on the outside of the building. I could have lied and told the client there was additional work and we needed to issue the contractor a change order. However, that would not have been consistent with our core values. So, I immediately walked into the client's office and informed him of my error and the additional cost, approximately $10,000, which was a huge sum of money for those days, still is. I informed him that

I would issue a credit for my services until that cost was covered. I'll never forget his response. "This is why I trust you so much. You could have lied to me, and I wouldn't have known. Thank you. This is why your team will be working here for the next ten years." As of the writing of this book, we have been there for twelve years, with at least another three years to go. We've also quadrupled the amount of services that we provide for them—honesty does get rewarded.

Another one of my favorite stories involves another favorite client. Our team was working on a building facade and missed some work that needed to be performed. Unfortunately, by the time our team noticed, the scaffold had already been removed, which significantly increased the cost of the mistake. Even more unfortunate, human nature kicked in when our team members initially spoke to the client, and they tried to come up with an excuse. As soon as I learned of it, I spoke with our team involved with the project, got the full story, and realized it was our mistake alone. I called the client immediately and admitted the mistake and that it was my responsibility; after all—something broke down on my team. The client immediately responded, "This is why I love you guys and will always work with you. I don't expect perfection; I just want honesty."

It is amazing how mistakes can build trust if you're willing to be vulnerable and own the mistake. Occasionally, it doesn't work out, and clients will not be forgiving. However, clients who have unrealistic expectations of perfection are likely clients you should fire anyway.

One of the benefits of sharing learning moments openly is we were quickly able to identify where we needed additional training. It also helped us realize that we needed to ramp up our quality control. Great quality control catches these mistakes before they go out the door. So, being willing to share this allowed us to continue to improve. Now, to be clear, I'm not advocating for accepting mistakes in product delivery. All companies, especially professional services firms, must have very high standards.

We certainly have incredibly high standards, and in order to achieve and maintain this, we have put in place a rigorous training process and a very thorough quality control process. Both of these can be quite expensive, but in my opinion, they are great investments for our growth. The cost of training new employees, as well as continually pushing existing team members to grow through in-house and external training, can be quite expensive, but the investment in having a highly trained team is well worth it.

> How do you view mistakes? Do you view them as learning moments? Are you comfortable sharing them with others?

Don't Over Apologize

I'm a firm believer in apologizing for my errors, and I make plenty of mistakes, so I get a lot of practice. I made so many that I even made mistakes while apologizing for mistakes. Early on, I made a mistake on a report to a client. I don't remember what that mistake was; I just remember the lesson I learned.

This was early on in the business and our relationship with this client. I provided the report and spoke to the client about it. During that call, they realized I had made a mistake. I immediately apologized and stated that I would correct the error and send the revised report. I then apologized again.

When I sent the revised report, I apologized a third time and then sent a follow-up email a few days later apologizing once more. AJ, my main point of contact for the client and a great guy, called me and said, "Stop apologizing. You correctly apologized when it was first pointed out and corrected the error. By continuing to apologize, you just keep reminding us about it, and you look weak." Ouch, that hurt, but he was right; it did make me look weak.

Clearly, he wasn't saying not to apologize for our errors but rather to apologize once or even twice and then move on.

Celebrating the Highs

Mistakes can feel like lows in the flow of business. Since it was important for us to create a positive work environment, we tried to remember to celebrate the wins whenever possible. In hindsight, I likely could've been much better. Like many entrepreneurs, my eyes were often focused down the road, so I didn't take as much time as I probably should've to celebrate. We had a Christmas party every year, our annual retreat, dinner to celebrate our anniversary, and occasional happy hours. These events are a great way to get together in a setting outside the normal work environment, and they were also a very organic way to see the growth in the company and the team.

Our first Christmas "party" was just Donna and me saddled up to a bar watching football. Although it was somewhat impromptu and very economical, it gave us a chance to look back over the year, laugh at some of the tough times, and talk about the recent momentum. It really gave us tremendous energy for the new year ahead. As the years went on, the Christmas party continued to have a casual feel but grew into more organized events in classier establishments. It was always fun seeing the increased size of the group over the years through the eyes of our team's significant others, as was watching the progression of the relationships as younger team members would bring their boyfriend/girlfriend one year, only to arrive just a few short years later with that same person as their spouse. In day-to-day work, I would sometimes lose sight of that, but these parties were always great for highlighting the personal growth of the team.

For our first anniversary dinner, we went to our favorite local steakhouse. It was a table for four: me, Mary Jo, Donna, and her husband, Vinny. It was a great night, but the company was far from a thriving business, so it was a tempered mood, at least for me anyway. By the time we were celebrating our third anniversary, we needed to use a private room at that same steakhouse. For the fourth anniversary, we couldn't fit in that room, so we needed to use their larger private room. By the fifth anniversary, we had outgrown the intimate steakhouse altogether and needed to look for a new venue, one of the many consequences of growth.

With this obvious very visible sign of business growth, you'd think I would've been feeling pretty satisfied, but the curse for many entrepreneurs is that we never feel settled. While I was very happy that we made it to that 5-year milestone, I shared with the team the often-repeated stat that 80 percent of all small businesses fail within the first five years, so congratulations to us, but I was quick to follow up with 80 percent of those that survive fail within the next five years. I likely should've kept that second part to myself.

Do you need help remembering to celebrate your wins? Who can you enlist, if necessary, to be your gauge and let you know when to celebrate them more frequently? Or less frequently?

Shut Down Christmas Week

Celebrating the highs was a clear pat on the back and felt great in the moment, but it often didn't have a long-lasting impact on recharging the batteries. A more subtle but more impactful way that we chose to reward ourselves at the end of a long but successful year was to shut down from Christmas Eve through New Year's Day. The seasonality of our niche was such that it followed a cyclical bell curve, with the winter being the slowest part of the year and work picking up through the spring and summer, which is our busiest part of the year. Work would start slowing down again from the fall to the winter, and the cycle would start all over again. So, we typically felt a good bit of fatigue near the end of November as projects would be wrapping up for the year.

One particular year, I personally felt it the most and thought the team might be feeling it too. So, I decided to shut the office down from Christmas Eve through January 2nd, fully paid. The intent, which worked tremendously, was to allow everyone to be with their loved ones, get some rest, and come back refreshed for the new year.

With the paid holidays of Christmas Eve and Day as well as New Year's Eve and Day, I was really only adding three additional paid days off but giving the team ten straight days off. Since the office would be closed and we all would be off at the same time, we would have very few work interruptions, proving to be much more valuable than typical PTO. We could all really disconnect, myself included. This worked so well the first year that we made this an annual benefit.

To help set ourselves up for success in the new year, we would trade three hours of work for three days off—it's amazing how much unnecessary "stuff" we can accumulate in one year. We would all spend one evening in the office before the Christmas break, cleaning and reorganizing. First, we worked through the common areas, conference rooms, file cabinets, closets, etc., and then each of us would attack our desks. We'd order pizzas and have a beer or two while keeping the mood light but incredibly productive.

The feeling we all had on January 2nd when we returned to a clean, organized office to start the new year was an incredible boost to morale and productivity. It was well worth the three days of revenue, especially since it was typically a slow month for revenue anyway.

All Entrepreneurs Should Coach Youth Sports

Colin Powell said, "Effective leaders are made, not born. They learn from trial and error and from experience." For me, that experience came from everywhere I could possibly find it. I absorbed every lesson that I could, including while coaching youth sports.

Coaching youth sports is a blast; I absolutely love it. It's also incredibly humbling and frustrating, just like entrepreneurship. The parallels between coaching, leading, and managing a youth sports team and a business are endless, and so are the lessons in becoming a better coach, leader, and manager. As such, I firmly believe that every entrepreneur should coach youth sports. In addition to the lessons learned, we can use a little more fun in our lives, and the forced mental break from our office is often just what we need. I can go to a really fun social event or really compelling educational presentation and still find my mind wandering back to work, but as a youth sports coach, I am dialed in for the entire game. It's a well-needed reprieve.

When I started coaching three-year-olds to play soccer, I realized how ineffective a communicator I was. If you speak too long to them and ramble on, they will simply sit down, walk away, or start talking to their friends. My employees may not have been that obvious on the outside, but more than likely, they were drifting off internally if, or more like when, I was rambling on. When I would have the soccer team huddled up nicely and ask that "someone go get the ball," they would *all* go get the ball. *Okay, noted. Be very specific about who you would like to get the ball and what you want them to do with that ball when they get it.* If you yell to a kid, "Run straight," they may, in fact, run straight, but not necessarily in the direction you hoped. *Okay, again noted, be more specific.* Anyone who has witnessed little guys play soccer knows it's called magnet ball for a reason. Wherever the ball goes, all of the kids on each team will go with it, even if that ball rolls two fields away. *So, clearly defined boundaries are important. Got it.*

I was coaching the basketball team for my sons, Dolan and Finn, a few years ago. We were holding our own against a team that was much better than us, or at least their coach clearly thought so. At halftime, he lined his boys up along the wall of the gym and screamed at them. Now, I've seen coaches yell many, many times, and I've been guilty myself of raising my voice more than I am proud of, but this was more like how I imagine a prison warden yells at inmates. I was trying to keep my boys focused, but of course, I couldn't, so I decided to lean into the spectacle. I asked the boys to all look over and watch the other team for a second, then pointed out that we were 100 percent going to win this game because those boys were going to play scared in the second half. Our boys went out in the second half, executed the fundamentals, had a lot of fun, and, of course, won. If our teams at work understand the game plan, are taught how to perform the fundamentals, and then are allowed to have some fun without fear of unjust punishment, no doubt they perform better.

As I write this book, one obvious parallel between business and youth sports comes from the best coach I ever had: my dad. As an immigrant from Ireland, he never played organized baseball; however, he coached my baseball team to several championships. He just needed to know how to teach us the fundamentals or recruit other dads who could, recognize talent for certain skills, and motivate us to learn and have fun.

Similarly to me, and likely you, he was a guy who worked a lot when we were kids. But as far as I can recall, somehow, he was at everything we needed him to be.

As my oldest son, Gavin, is now out of youth sports, he and I are coaching several of the other kids' teams together. Coaching one or two of my kids *with* one of my kids just magnifies the joy *and* the learning. For example, I've learned, slower than I should have, that the kids respond better to him. They'll take feedback and guidance differently from him than they will from me. Since he's much closer to having played the sport, he also remembers a lot more of the drills and techniques than I do. So, I've learned to sit back and let him work his magic. I've stepped more into an advisor's role: he bounces questions off of me, we discuss strategy, and then he executes. It doesn't take much to draw the analogy to our employees and how we should support them as they take on additional responsibilities and transition into leadership.

As coaches, we learn to laugh at ourselves and not to take ourselves too seriously. Whether we win or lose an individual game doesn't really matter. What matters is that we improved and that we all want to come back again next week, next season, etc.

It's more obvious with toddlers, but it is equally important with players and employees of all ages: a good night's rest, as well as proper hydration and food intake, is critical to success. Toddlers will get water in the middle of an at-bat because they're thirsty. We as adults will stop and laugh, but deep down, we should recognize that sometimes games/practices run long, and if we want our players to be at their best, we should allow for breaks. Similarly, some of our work days are long, and some of our individual meetings run long. If we want our employees to be at their best, we should allow for water/snack breaks. We may not need gushers and orange slices at work meetings, but the concept of nourishing our team is solid (and kid-approved).

Regardless of how good or bad a practice or game was, kids will want to hug a friend, wave to their parents, and get ice cream afterward. Similarly, our coworkers can regain that youthful smile and energy through a simple conversation with a work friend, a call with a loved one, and/or an after-work drink. We should embrace that.

Meg Meeker

In addition to absorbing as much as I could about being a better business leader, I also wanted to learn as much as I could about being a good dad and raising great kids.

I was introduced to Meg Meeker, a pediatrician turned author and parenting guru, through Dave Ramsey's podcasts. Meg's books were great resources for me to learn how to be the best parent I could be, but they also helped to minimize some of the guilt that the late nights at the office had on me. The first two books of Meg's that I read were *Boys Should Be Boys* and *Strong Fathers Strong Daughters*. Both provide great practical wisdom about how to instill values into our kids, how to handle social media, attempt to ensure they develop a love of God, and how to understand and communicate with them as they mature.

Meg shares that kids often look back on quality time with their parents as being much bigger, longer lasting, and more frequent than they actually were. I never used this as an excuse to skip out on events, but it helped knowing that, hopefully, my efforts weren't going unnoticed by them. Whether it was an evening practice after school or a weekend morning, the youth sports routine in our house was usually the same: I would race from the office to the field or gym, meet Mary Jo and the kids there, coach their youth sports teams, and then race back to the office. As I talk with our older kids now, the reality is they don't really remember the running around in the early years; they just remember that I was there coaching, always.

Now that my schedule has adjusted to be more in line with our values, I love the time in the car with the younger kids to and from sports as much as I do the time coaching, but the point is at least I had that time coaching the older kids in the early days.

Is what you're reading and listening to diverse enough to cover all aspects of the Entrepreneurial Trinity? Where do you need to shift your focus more: faith, family, or business?

Dear Brian,

The first few years of the business were certainly a whirlwind. Three years had come and gone in a literal blink of an eye. We welcomed our little man Dolan into the world. We brought him home from the hospital on a Sunday, and you were back to work the following day, that Monday. The company was growing, and you slowing down just didn't seem like an option. You working seven days a week was now our family norm, and the kids were young, so they had grown accustomed to that. About two months after Dolan was born, I asked you if we could take the kids away for a night, and you agreed. We drove out to Great Wolf Lodge in Pennsylvania, and it was amazing. Just to see the kids cracking up and going on all those crazy slides and water rides with you was fantastic. It was incredible to see us as a family unit, and we wanted more of it. I think that little overnight was somewhat of an awakening for the two of us. We realized we needed to put more emphasis on getting away with the kids and not going as long as we did without a vacation.

In those early days, going away for more than a night or two or anywhere other than a few hour car ride away was not an option, and that was okay. It was not in our budget, and there was no way you could be away from the office for more than two or three days. But again, we just needed to create our family moments around the business's current situation. You became extremely intentional about this, babe. Thank you! Among all the other seats you were holding in the company, you now took the seat of our family vacation coordinator, and you still are today!

We spent the next two years strategically placing a few overnights throughout the calendar year. We took trips to Hershey Park and Kalahari water park, and our anniversary go-to became a night at Crystals Springs Spa. None of these destinations were more than a three-hour drive from our home, and all locked in some unforgettable family time and memories.

Placing emphasis on family vacations became so important to you and me. These mini overnights early on with the kids and with each other gave us a glimpse of how fantastic that uninterrupted time together really was. They fueled us to want more of that. We'd return from our trips recharged and ready to go, ready to work hard so we could get more family time and more time with each other.

To date, we've been blessed to travel to some pretty amazing destinations all over the world with our crew and with each other. Having been given that gift of time with the kids and you are memories we will cherish forever. Thank you, Brian, for saying yes to that little overnight at Great Wolf Lodge over 11 years ago. And thank you for your intentionality to get away with us as frequently as the business and our budget would allow.

I love you,
MJ

Hey Mary Jo,

As I think back on the early years of our family and our business, I see how our strong faith subconsciously impacted every aspect of both.

While we did go to church most Sundays and holy days and sent our kids to Catholic school, we weren't the couple who said the rosary every day, at least not until Mark Wahlberg made it cool. We were, though, the type of couple who allowed our decisions to be informed by our beliefs. We attempted to continue to follow and be inspired by religious leaders and couples, and when the chips were down—especially when the chips were down—we did find our way into a church for a weekday mass or just a stop in to ask God for wisdom and grace.

The subconscious impact of our faith is displayed throughout this chapter through the importance of honesty and integrity, which has always been huge for us both. The level of honesty that results in (vulnerably) admitting mistakes builds trust and growth in relationships and individuals. Seeking that honesty creates wisdom and humility, which also creates growth and improvement.

As difficult as it may sometimes be to live out our faith, we have both reaped the rewards of it tenfold. In business alone, the growth that came from ourselves and our team members due to honest feedback and the loyalty we built with our team, our clients, and our industry partners through profound integrity resulted in increased revenue and profit. Most of all, the peace that came with knowing that we were doing the right thing, or at least trying our best to do the right thing, is transformational.

I suppose that is why honesty and integrity are mentioned so frequently in the Bible, which is often referred to as the best business book of all time.

Love,
Brian

IV
ADOLESCENCE

Whoever loves discipline loves knowledge, but those who hate to be rebuked are stupid.

—Proverbs 12:1

Just like a small child whose legs have become strong and stable, a young business is growing and ready to take off. With the firm foundation established, the business begins branching out and establishing its own identity.

Children begin school, make friends, explore activities, and develop unique personalities. So, too, does the business. More team members are hired to meet the growing needs of new clients, additional coaching is required to expand the leadership knowledge and professional connections, and new areas of business expansion start to become real. The learning that primarily occurred in-house now happens equally outside the home or business.

The hard work put in during the early stages—core values, right hires, right-fit clients—allows the business to move to the next stage of growth: adolescence.

NYC Office

As we continued to grow our team, we decided it was time to open an office in New York City. It made sense from the perspective of serving our clients, who were mostly located in NYC. It also allowed us to recruit professionals from all areas surrounding NYC, as opposed to just Northwest of the city, where our New Jersey office was located.

Looking for office space in Manhattan was a very different experience from looking for space in suburban New Jersey, but it was a similar test of my confidence. Although we had experienced some success and growth, the larger expense and longer lease duration terms in NYC were testing my confidence in our growth projections. On the other hand, the allure of some of the building addresses was very attractive and tested my ego.

I remember talking to my very good friend, Brian Isaacson, who is a fantastic real estate attorney, about a space down on Wall Street that I had looked at. I explained to him the size of the space and the terms of the lease. Brian knew our growth projections and pointed out the very obvious issue that we would grow out of that space in four years (in his opinion, two to three years), and the lease was a 10-year term. As I defended my mindset, I knew immediately he was right, and I was losing a battle against both my ego and self-confidence. And, as it turned out, he was right; we would've grown out of that space in less than three years.

After the conversation with Brian, we adjusted our plans and looked exclusively for co-working spaces that would allow us to adjust the amount of space we needed as we grew until we leveled off our NYC employee growth. We ended up renting space from WeWork in Times Square on the corner of 41st Street and Broadway. This was a much better geographic location for us, which was a factor that I wasn't taking into account with the allure of the Wall Street address.

WeWork is a co-working space with very flexible monthly lease terms and the ability to move to new larger/smaller spaces within the same building as business needs evolve. Our initial WeWork office was set up for two people to report there while the rest of the team remained at our New Jersey office. We quickly moved to a four-person office, and shortly after, we took a space for eight people, and eventually, we had enough space for seventeen people. We accomplished this all within the same building, so our physical and mailing addresses never changed.

As a side note, the Times Square address was nice for the ego as well. Not all pride is bad; sometimes, walking a little taller because of accomplishments helps fuel belief in continued growth.

Although we now had an NYC office that made sense strategically and financially, I still had some head trash around having an unconventional co-working space. I was concerned about what clients would think of the mindset as well as the visual appearance and layout if they came to visit. As it turned out, many understood the logic and appreciated it. Additionally, the few clients that visited our office back then loved the amenities available, including the various meeting spaces and conference rooms. Some even used those conference rooms for meetings instead of hosting in their own offices.

Years later, when we started to outgrow the 17-person space in WeWork, it became clear financially and strategically that it was time to rent a more conventional office space, which was much larger and in a much better strategic location than that original Wall Street space that I coveted.

Who is your Brian Isaacson?
Who are your trusted friends/advisers who will help you make wise decisions when your emotions are conflicting with your own logic?

"Obligatory" Vacations

In 2015, we took our first two real vacations, which may not have happened if not for two great milestones.

In July, we went to Ireland for two weeks to celebrate my parents' 50th wedding anniversary. In the weeks before we left, I spent a lot of time preparing for the trip to get myself and my team ready. But I didn't let my team know that I didn't want or need updates and would prefer only to be called in emergencies. As a result, I found myself getting involved in issues that I didn't need to be involved in, which then prevented me from being fully present with the family.

It would've been smart to have done a test run of a few days off, with no contact with the office, to see how things would go and adjust any processes before this important trip. As a result, I received more phone calls during my trip to Ireland than I wished and had a hard time unplugging.

Later that year, we went to China for two weeks to bring home our son Finn, who was adopted from Beijing. As a result of lessons learned and documented from the trip to Ireland, I did a much better job delegating and communicating with my team before going and was more confident in my team's ability while I was gone. That, combined with a timezone difference and the stress of the adoption, resulted in significantly less work stress on that trip.

We later used those lessons when our VP of ops, Kevin, was going to Australia and New Zealand for his honeymoon. We knew that we wouldn't want him disturbed while on his honeymoon, so we had Kevin take some practice days in advance, working from home but completely disconnecting from the team. This worked much better for all involved.

Strategic Coach®, a coaching program that I'll share more about later in this chapter, takes this concept even further with Free, Focus, and Buffer Days®, which are part of The Entrepreneurial Time System and are meant to be days with no communication with the team. Free Days are spent doing what we love, and Focus Days are spent doing the three things that only we can do to bring the most value to the business. Strategic Coach recommends 150 Free Days per year. Of course, that includes weekends. But for many of us, the number of true Free Days we were taking was a fraction of that prior to learning how to delegate effectively. As I started taking proper Free Days and Focus Days, I witnessed exactly what Strategic Coach taught us: My team could and would step up to handle many of the responsibilities that I was handling on a day-to-day basis. And to be honest, they did a much better job at it. Many of my team loved those new responsibilities and were much more naturally gifted at them. Taking Free Days was a game changer because once I delegated these tasks, I did so permanently and didn't take them back. If they needed to move to somebody else, fine, but they didn't come back to me as the entrepreneur.

I often think about how the first few years would've been different if I had embraced, or even self-enforced, the Free Day concept. I won't pretend that I would've taken 150 Free Days that first year, but 104 Free Days should've been easy. Establishing a goal of 104 sets the mindset of being completely unplugged every Saturday and Sunday. But it also allows some wiggle room, knowing that with ten holidays in a year, if I "needed" to work a Saturday or even ten, I still would have hit the goal of 104. Also, had I prioritized taking a vacation, even a staycation, that would be five more Saturdays I could work if I "needed" to.

For many reasons, we are so grateful that those two milestones occurred when they did, which "forced" me to take legitimate vacations. Those vacations proved that the company could run without my everyday presence. Without those obligatory vacations, who knows how long it would've been before I allowed myself to take a proper vacation.

How many Free Days have you taken in the past year? What's preventing you from taking more? Who can assist you with taking more?

Dear Brian,

Adoption was something we talked about early on during our dating days. We both felt a strong connection to it and knew it was largely in part of our earlier days of volunteering, myself in Haiti and you in Honduras. Throughout our time volunteering, our eyes were opened to a world we didn't know existed. Through the children we met on those trips, we returned home different people, awakened souls, if you will. Mr. Russo, my philosophy teacher from Molloy, said it perfectly: You think you are going to volunteer and bring value and help to those in need, and that you do, but the value you receive from your experience is tenfold, immeasurable, and it doesn't leave you ever!

Dolan, our fourth, was only about three months old, and the business was growing at a steady, rapid rate. I had cut down my hours further at the hospital at this point to per-diem, doing about 3–4 shifts a month. This helped to accommodate the kid's growing schedule with school and activities, as well as alleviate some of the burden for my mom and your parents, who would watch the children for us. One evening, I approached you and told you I thought it was time that we start fulfilling our promise to ourselves that we would one day adopt a child. You wholeheartedly agreed, and your excitement and enthusiasm drove me to start doing my due diligence in looking into adoption programs and agencies. I had work the following morning, and into the treatment room walked this beautiful woman in her early 30s. We got to chatting about our children, and she asked me if I'd like to see a picture of her sons. I responded absolutely, and she showed me a picture of the two most beautiful little boys. I told her they were gorgeous and she quickly opened up how she adopted them, two little brothers, from Ethiopia. I thought, Wow, God, you must have really been waiting for Brian and me to get going on our adoption journey to place this woman right in front of me the morning after our discussion. She told me about the amazing adoption agency she and her husband had used and what a beautiful experience she had with them. I contacted the agency the next day, and our application was submitted to their Ethiopia program within days. I was off and running with the list of forms and paperwork that needed to be completed—it's funny how your passion and drive seem to go hand in hand. It took us just shy of three months to complete everything. After meeting with our amazing social worker, Stephen, to complete our home study, we were officially accepted into Ethiopia's program.

Within two weeks of our acceptance, our agency closed down its Ethiopia program. Effective immediately, they were no longer performing adoptions out of Ethiopia. We were devastated and extremely discouraged. Everything was lining up. God, how could this happen? Now, you and I are very rational people, and in our minds, we understood the severity of the situation that ensued, causing our agency to halt adoptions from the country, but our hearts felt rejected. We met with Stephen, our social worker, at our dining room table shortly after to review our next steps. Now, I forgot to mention that Stephen is one of the coolest people Brian and I have ever met. He's this tall, super chill, and relaxed man who just has this amazing charisma about him; he's aided countless families with their adoption journey/journeys, truly a man out there doing God's work. He looked across the table at yours and my dejected eyes and said, "Guys, this is about a child, not a country. What about China?" Just like that, he blurted it out so matter of factly. You, Brian, who rarely does not have immediate feedback, sat silent. We both just sat there absorbing his words. Stephen's words resonated, and we switched our dossier over to China.

The agency we utilized maintained a beautiful list of "waiting children." This list was compiled of children, most of whom had special needs or who were older, or sibling groups that needed to find their forever families. It wasn't an easy site to go through. Now, I do not mean ease of use; I mean emotionally. I remember scrolling through and seeing Finn's little face. He looked petrified in the picture, only two years old at the time, but something drew me in. Stephen had put us in touch with a family that had adopted a little girl from China, and I remember asking the mom how she knew this particular little girl was the "one," the one who was meant to be their daughter. And I remember her answer; she said she just looked familiar. And that was it, that was exactly it when I saw Finn's tiny, scared face; he just looked familiar—he looked like our son. I showed you his picture, and you couldn't have agreed more. It's funny; I remember showing my mom a picture of Finn when we shared the news with the kids and our parents that we were adopting him. My mom said, "He has his dad's smile, meaning you, Brian." So I guess yes, he just looked familiar to us! We were matched with Finn in March, and all six of us—you and I and the four kids—traveled to Beijing, China, in November to bring our beautiful little man home.

Now, I'd be remiss in this part of my letter to you if I didn't mention the business's role in our adoption journey. Not only did the business's success at the time allow us to use a premier not-for-profit agency for Finn's adoption, but it also permitted the six of us to travel to Beijing to bring him home. The leadership you had put in place allowed you to leave the country and travel to China for two and a half weeks. The company's leadership also allowed you to disconnect and fully embrace this amazing time in China with our family and our newest addition, our son Finn. After only five years since the business's creation, this was a pretty remarkable feat you had accomplished with your company. Naturally, there were phone calls to be made, emails to send, and virtual meetings that had to be attended, but this was extremely minimal, especially when comparing it to the work-related stress you experienced while on our family trip to Ireland only six months prior. You returned home from Ireland not so much frustrated with your team but more so of how could we improve this moving forward, your approach to most things in life, Brian. You and your team put different processes and parameters in place, and our seamless trip to China was proof of your team's solid leadership. I won't say the trip was completely stress-free, but your stress came from constantly counting five little Sullivan heads in a crowded Tiananmen Square in Beijing rather than from the business office.

Thank you for your heart, Brian, for having the vision to create the business, for working incredibly hard to provide this opportunity to our family, and most of all, for bringing our son home to us. The joy, love, and compassion Finn has brought into our family is unsurmountable. I pray that he is continuously blessed throughout his entire life for all the blessings he has bestowed upon you and me.

I love you, Brian,
MJ

EOS®

In 2015, our team consisted of myself and ten people between our two offices, who all reported directly to me in a relatively flat structure. While we had some solid early growth from 2010's meager revenue of $11,000 to $1.9MM in 2015, we had certainly hit a revenue plateau the past few years with revenue of $1.3M, $1.6MM and $1.9MM in 2013, 2014, and 2015, respectively. We knew this wasn't the way to proceed forward and grow a successful firm. However, I hadn't seen a way that I liked and had yet to determine how I wanted to grow the structure.

Mike Frech brought in a book called *Traction*© by Gino Wickman, which his wife recommended. We both read it over the weekend and immediately knew that this was something that could help solve many of our issues. Traction defines the Entrepreneurial Operating System©, also known as EOS. Mike's wife, Sue, had recommended a coach named Mark O'Donnell. We brought Mark in to help us implement EOS for our team.

At the time, it was a relatively large financial investment for us, but a bigger investment in time. Looking back now, the return on that investment was tremendous. It is likely the single best business decision that I made, and, as you'll see, it led to a cascading series of decisions related to education investments that paid off significantly in several different ways.

The Entrepreneurial Operating System helped us clearly define our vision, goals, responsibilities, and values. Additionally, it provided the ability to have consistent, clear, and concise meetings that went straight to the issues by separating the issue to be solved from the people associated with the issue, so it became less personal. To be clear, the concepts in EOS are easy to understand, but it took a lot of courage and confidence on the leadership side and a lot of convincing to our team members because it added more responsibilities and meetings. But in doing so, it provided a tremendous amount of clarity and focus.

Core Values

One of the first things Mark walked us through as our implementer was establishing our core values. Through what was a relatively fun process, we fairly quickly identified the values that we held core to our beliefs as a leadership team. Since the objective is to then hire, fire, review, reward, and recognize based on those core values, we had to make sure that they were accurate. So, we tested them against ourselves and evaluated each leadership team member against those values. This was definitely not a fun portion of the process. It can be uncomfortable, but it quickly highlights the level and importance of full transparency. Fortunately, our leadership team faired well in our initial assessment.

Sharing these core values with the team and then measuring each other and all future hires by the values proved to be even more powerful than I initially thought it would be. As an example, several years after rolling out EOS, we hired a very accomplished professional in our industry who, honestly, was a big deal for our small team to be able to recruit. Our interview process involved at least three separate interviews. During the first and third interviews, a significant amount of time was devoted to discussing the values in great detail and emphasizing the fact that we take them very, very seriously. Well, this professional was clearly not a core values match from the start. To be fair, we had six core values. If someone doesn't align with our values, it certainly doesn't make them a bad person; it just means they'll be unhappy working with us and vice versa. That certainly was the case in this situation. One of our six values is Team First, and this individual was more of a lone wolf. This led to immediate frustrations from the start. However, because we could easily discuss the issue of whether or not she was exhibiting the core value of being Team First, it allowed for a very rapid decision to part ways and saved both sides a lot of time and frustration. In her exit interview, when we asked why she would join the team knowing that she preferred to be a lone wolf and we had spent so much time talking about our core values during the interview process, she responded, "Every business talks about values and puts them up on the wall, but nobody actually enforces them." That sentiment right there may be a very sad reality for many businesses, but for us, it just reinforced why we should stay true to our core values and, furthermore, how they contributed to our success.

Vision

As we grew the business, it became more and more important for me to have the confidence to share the original vision that I had established back in the public library in 2010 and allow that vision to evolve. Fortunately, clearly defining the vision for the organization is a key component of EOS. Having the full leadership team involved in the discussion of the vision created significantly more buy-in from the leaders and the rest of the team. We used a simple two-page business plan to share the vision with the team. This was simply one sheet of paper identifying the key components of the Vision on the front and the more granular objectives on the back of the page.

With projected revenue of $1.9MM for 2015, we set a vision for 2025 of $13.5MM in revenue. Sharing this with the team certainly led to a lot of questions and some justifiable uncertainty; however, it also sent the signal of a great deal of opportunity. Rolling out the vision highlighted the team members who fully embraced the big goal and understood the why behind it.

Similar to core values, the mission or purpose of a business can be incredibly powerful if it is real and an actual guide for decision-making, not just a slogan on a website. Through EOS, we established our Purpose as To Empower Others to Improve their Quality of Life. While this may seem like a lofty goal for a small niche engineering firm, to our team, it was a driving force. When we thought of our purpose, we thought of empowering each other by creating growth in the organization to allow for new opportunities and increased compensation. We also thought about improving the quality of life of each other's loved ones by providing a place to work that had reasonable work-life balance expectations and emphasized personal growth for each team member. Additionally, we attempted to improve the quality of life of our clients and industry partners by creating trusted relationships built on profound integrity. Lastly, we improved the quality of life of those in need through our generous charitable contributions and community service.

Rocks

To further clarify the Vision, we established several tiers of long-term goals. At a high level, we had three very basic goals to accomplish within the next 10 years; typically, these were based on our revenue, employee count, and impact on others. Additionally, we had a much longer, more granular list of 3-year goals that included the same metrics in the 10-year goals as well as items like "open an office in a new target market," "have ten new national clients," and "no client at >10 percent total revenue." In my experience, some team members could easily see the 10-year goals as being attainable, but most first needed to gain confidence via the 3-year goals to buy in.

We all know that to tackle really big goals, we must break them down into smaller, more manageable pieces. So, the 3-year goals are further broken down with the five+/- goals that need to be accomplished within the next year to set ourselves on the right path to accomplish the 3 and 10-year goals. This provided more clarity and allowed for course correction along the way to ensure we stayed in line as we worked towards the bigger vision. Breaking the 1-year goals down further into quarterly "Rocks" results in goals that are much more actionable. The reason they are called Rocks comes from the parable in Stephen Covey's book, *First Things First*, of the rocks, the pebbles, and the sand.[5]

Each quarter, everyone on our team identified three individual Rocks that were the most important goals they could accomplish for the team that quarter. At least one of those Rocks had to support one of the larger company Rocks. The power that comes from intentionally aligning individual Rocks with the company's larger Rocks was incredible. That, combined with the increased accountability that resulted from each individual having the freedom to choose their own rock and then discuss it with the team, is transformative.

Processes

Although I'm an engineer, the discussion of processes in *Traction* is what gave me the most pause. I did not want to create a company of robots; I felt that we had a team of very intelligent people, and I didn't want to restrict their intellect. Once we realized the intent was not to document 100 percent of every task but to follow the 20/80 rule of documenting the 20 percent of a process that produces 80 percent of the results, I was more convinced.

Once we started documenting and rolling out our core processes, I became a firm believer and even advocate for adhering to them. Many on the team similarly embraced the processes, which created a path to accomplish projects effectively while still allowing creativity. The processes also provided an efficient way to onboard and train new team members.

Scoreboard

Metrics are a vital tool to identify issues in an organization, but as we learned (the hard way), if you calculate your metrics wrong or are measuring the wrong data altogether, you'd potentially be better off with none. As Mark used to say to us, "Would you rather be flying a plane with a broken instrument panel or no instrument panel at all?" The correct answer is no instrument panel at all because at least you would know that you needed to rely on your visual field and other resources, whereas if you have a broken instrument panel, you may think that your plane is headed where it should be going and is safe, but in reality, you could be way off course.

The use of a scoreboard to measure the past thirteen weeks helped us identify issues relatively quickly. Reviewing the Scorecard weekly helped ensure that we were measuring the right data and tracking the quarterly and annual results against expectations. It also ensured that we were calculating the metrics correctly and not relying on a broken instrument panel.

One particular example that illustrates the power of good metrics and a thorough scoreboard was our field report turnaround time. It was important to us (and our clients) that we send field reports out the door within two days of a site visit. This was a challenge for sure, but it was doable with the right processes in place.

Prior to having a thorough scoreboard in place, we were inconsistent across our team, and conversations around this item were very vague. For example: "Your turnaround time seems slow." Once a scoreboard was in place, we were able to easily identify individual turnaround times for each team member and then have very productive conversations on ways to improve.

In one such case, one of our engineers was attempting to accommodate the contractors we deal with by spending two straight days in the field and then coming into the office to write field reports. This was putting immense stress on her and on the other members of the team who were part of the process. Once the engineer realized that if she just tweaked her schedule a little, she could easily make the desired turnaround time. Within two weeks, she was one of the most efficient on the team at turning around reports and, more importantly, was much less stressed.

Delegation

As previously mentioned, accountability is a tremendous byproduct of EOS, so much so that the organization chart in an EOS-run business is thoroughly developed to clearly define what each role or seat in the organization is accountable for. When setting it up, we identified the roles we needed and the items that each seat would be accountable for and *then* determined who would sit in those seats. Prior to this exercise, I had often seen individuals move into roles they were not suited for simply because they were the best at their current roles. Dave Ramsey describes the analogy of the bank teller who is the best teller in her branch and then is promoted to branch manager, which requires a totally different skill set. After struggling as a branch manager for several months, she is eventually let go. We've all seen this play out in many different businesses with many different areas of expertise. To combat this, we had a strong focus on attempting to delegate away as many of the tasks that any individual in the organization didn't love doing and wasn't great at

We had each team member create a list of all the tasks that they performed on a regular basis, divided up into four quadrants. The upper left is the tasks that the individual loves doing and is great at, and the upper right is the items they like doing and are good at. The bottom half is items they either don't like doing but are still good at or don't like doing and are not good at. By *honestly* organizing tasks into these four quadrants, it becomes more clear who belongs in which seats in the organization.

I emphasized the word honestly because it's sometimes difficult for people to admit what they are not good at or don't love doing. For me as an engineer and the owner of an engineering firm, it took me several iterations of my delegation lists over several years to admit that I don't love the technical review of documents. Once I did, we found two people on our team who loved doing it and were much better at it than I was. All this time, I was "falling on the sword," performing work I didn't love because I assumed nobody else did either. Once I saw the success those two had in taking on that role, I very quickly started delegating away more of the work that I didn't love.

Combining this delegation process with Strategic Coach's Impact Filter™ helped me transition away from "drive-by delegation." I'm not sure who came up with that term, but I love it. Drive-by delegation perfectly summed up my style for too many years. However, eventually, I learned what I should delegate and how to delegate it.

The more I learned to embrace what I'm uniquely gifted at and love doing and learned to effectively delegate away the rest, the better my team performed and the more joy and energy I've had at work and at home.

The delegation process we used was not just a great tool for me but also for the rest of my team. We had regular conversations with each team member about what they were delegating away as well as the work they loved doing and could, therefore, now take on more of. As a result, we were able to provide feedback and more accurately identify new responsibilities and sometimes new roles for our team.

Gino Wickman characterizes ideal team members in *Traction* as the right people in the right seats. It was our experience that finding the Right People, those who are a core value match and embrace the company vision and culture, was one of our biggest challenges. So, if we had the right person in the wrong seat, we worked hard to find the right seat for them. Changing roles comes with uncertainty and insecurity, but using the delegation mindset helped us eliminate some of the uncertainty. This allowed us to move many different team members throughout their tenure to more and more specialized roles where they excelled while doing the work they loved.

Weekly Meetings

The meeting cadence defined in EOS is intimidating at first, but it is an effective way to allow all voices to be heard, ensure that the most important topics are discussed in order of priority, and guarantee that meetings start on time and *end on time*. The magic of the meeting occurs when the team collectively Identifies, Discusses, and Solves issues. The goal of the meeting agenda is to get to this portion of the meeting quickly and then take the majority of the time to understand the issues and solve them.

The biggest negative side effect of running a business on EOS for so many years is that I often find meetings that aren't run efficiently unbearable. Dancing around important items, leaving them to the end, or simply not respecting the team's time to end a meeting on schedule used to bother me, but now, it's downright painful.

In *Death By Meeting,* Patrick Lencioni states: "When a group of intelligent people come together to talk about issues that matter, it is both natural and productive for disagreement to occur. Resolving those issues is what makes a meeting productive, engaging, even fun." Most people who were on our team would agree that once they were used to the cadence of the meetings and understood the importance of the high level of accountability, the results were tremendous, the opportunities for the team were ever-expanding, and we definitely had a lot of fun.

In fact, many people who worked for our team or others running on EOS shared with me that operating on EOS is like having a light turned on in a previously dark room. Business becomes much easier when you can clearly see the obstacles and opportunities.

What resources will you use to develop the right operating system for your business? Have you found the one that resonates with you the most? Do you prefer a detailed business plan or a condensed single sheet?

Strategic Coach

To elevate the business even more, I joined Strategic Coach, a fantastic coaching program for entrepreneurs co-founded by Dan

Sullivan, no relation. Their coaching encourages us to measure backward against ourselves and our own growth quarterly to see whether or not we're happy with the progress.

During my first session in their Chicago office, our cohort of 60 business owners was asked to write down some of the biggest wins we had since starting our entrepreneurial journey. They said, if you're looking back ten years, five years, whatever it might be, to today, would you be happy with your progress? And inevitably, all of us said, "Yeah, sure, we'd be thrilled." And then they asked a very pointed question: "Then why aren't we?" So true. And that question hits hard because, as high achievers, we all continue to strive to grow and improve. But with that comes the fact that we're never quite satisfied. In Coach, they talk about the concept of the ideal future. As high achievers, we are constantly growing what our ideal future looks like as our capabilities grow.

As we start to accomplish some success, we inevitably dream bigger. And therefore, we never reach that ideal future. It's a concept called The Gap And The Gain® that Dan Sullivan talks about in the same-titled book, where we end up in this gap between where we currently are and our ideal future because the ideal future keeps growing.[6] If we don't look back quarterly at the gains we've made, we could end up in some really dark places.

So, in that first session of Coach, they asked us to write down our successes. Then they asked, "Who here struggles with self-confidence?" I started to raise my hand slowly, tentatively. I looked around the room and saw that just about everybody else was doing the same thing. And sure enough, as we all looked around and smiled, humbly laughing, we all raised our hands with more confidence.

Our coach that day, Chad Johnson, talked about The 4 C's Formula®: confidence, commitment, capability, and courage.[7] Then, they asked us to break up into groups to introduce ourselves and share about our businesses, our families, and the wins we wrote down.

In my group were the two guys who happened to be sitting next to me. One was this really nice, soft-spoken chiropractor with three offices, all in buildings that he owns. The guy on my right also had a great business with 200+ employees and was doing really well. At the end of the group session, we had a little time to kill, and I noticed that the guy on my right had a college football ring on his finger.

As a sports fan, I asked some really probing questions and learned that he won two national championships while in college and then went on to play in the NFL for nine years. Very few people make it to the NFL; a tiny fraction of those make it for nine years. I was completely shocked by this humble guy sitting next to me. He had this immense professional success and this immense sports success. Then, it dawned on me that he raised his hand to the self-confidence question. I was baffled to see that someone who had accomplished so much could also suffer from self-confidence issues, just like I do, and apparently, the rest of the room of very successful entrepreneurs.

Unfortunately, we often measure ourselves sideways against each other. I should look at the growth others have had and be inspired and happy for them. I should look at the growth that I've had and be happy for myself. Years later when relaying this story to high school students, a thought popped into my head: "Never measure sideways." Measure backward against yourself. If you're happy with your progress, great, keep going; if you're not, simply course correct and surge ahead.

I've learned, or should I say I'm still learning, that there will always be people smarter, faster, or stronger. That's not a new mantra. There will always be people who have a faster-growing business, a more profitable, bold business, and the type of clients that I want. Or maybe they have a smaller business that they're happier in, have more control of, and have a better profit margin. If I dwell on what they have going for them, I'm measuring sideways.

So, I've learned to measure backward for myself and analyze what I truly want, knowing that I cannot have it all, and then be content to tip my cap to them on their strengths.

Another game-changing concept that we worked on at Strategic Coach was attempting to discover our Unique Ability®. By using self-discovery, behavioral assessments, and input from friends and colleagues, we attempted to discover what we're most passionate about and what we are uniquely gifted at.

Sitting and really evaluating our self-assessments plus what we determined to be our strengths was a very powerful exercise, but what really magnified the experience for me was obtaining feedback from the people whose opinions mattered the most to me. It was a strange experience for me to send an email asking those closest to me to assess me and tell me what they think my unique ability is. It feels like a burden, it feels nervy, and mostly, it just feels weird.

That feeling subsided when I started to receive their responses; I was floored. To receive emails from a vast array of loved ones: family members, friends, including my boys from college, as well as professional colleagues, all with very similar feedback, I started to believe. Prior to that, as with most people, I dismissed my unique skills, thinking everyone could do it because it came easy to me. Once I finally honed in on my Unique Ability® and started sharing it with people, having in-depth conversations with them about it, I came to the realization that I should lean into it more. So here it goes:

> *My Unique Ability is to relate to and motivate others with profound integrity and humility to inspire growth beyond our own expectations.*

It initially felt strange sharing that with people, but the more I did and the more I heard them respond, "Yeah, that's it, that's you," the more I embraced it and focused my day-to-day responsibilities on it, and the more fun I had.

What is your Unique Ability?
What is it you love doing that comes so effortlessly that you assume it's easy for everyone? Are you willing to lean into it?
Are you willing to embrace your God-given talent?

To discover your Unique Ability, I highly suggest you read *Unique Ability 2.0 Discovery: Define Your Best Self.*

Farm Club

As we continued to grow, we recognized we needed more concentrated business development efforts. So, we began to measure the volume of work that we performed with existing clients and identified our Top 20 Farm Club®. As the name implies, these were our top 20 clients by revenue. We wanted to make sure we knew who these clients were and what the common traits they shared were. The goal was to make sure that we appropriately nurtured the relationship to ensure that these clients remained happy with our services and, hopefully, would continue to give us more projects. We made sure that we had others on the team checking in with these clients in addition to the engineers who were assigned to their projects. This showed the client that we truly cared about exceeding their expectations and gave them ample opportunity to communicate any concerns or frustrations they had. Although the intent of these routine check-ins was to ensure the client was happy and to get out in front of any issues, the typical result was actually just a quick five-minute phone call that would often lead to new opportunities.

In addition to identifying and nurturing the top 20, we wanted to find other clients just like them, so to that end, we created a separate list called our Farm Club. Here, we kept the names of the companies and individuals that we were targeting and hoped would one day become one of our top 20. Again, we ensured we had regular conversations with them if we already had a relationship. If we didn't, we made it our mission to get to know those clients. These days, it can be very difficult to get in front of prospective clients, so keeping our Farm Club list and knowing detailed information about the clients on that list allowed us to be very intentional. We were purposeful in which industry events we attended, and when meeting with networking colleagues, we were prepared with the names of those we specifically wanted to meet.

Initially, many of the potential clients on the Farm Club seemed out of reach to some on our team; however, as we started landing work with these Farm Club clients, our team became more confident, and our potential target clients became more ambitious.

The Bench

Recruitment was always a challenge. We certainly were not the only company facing that issue, but as a relatively new, relatively small company in our niche, it seemed particularly hard. One method we used to help overcome that issue we referred to as "The Bench." This was a list of people we knew or were referred to us, who we felt could be a core values match and fit well on our team. Most of the time, when the right person came along, we would hire them even if we weren't looking at the time, knowing that as we continued to grow, we would need them. Occasionally, though, we just couldn't swing it in the budget, so their name would be added to The Bench.

We weren't a fan of poaching people from other companies for several reasons, so we tried to avoid that. So, most of the names on the bench were people that we knew, but they hadn't expressed interest in leaving their current job. The key people on our team knew who was on The Bench, so if someone got wind that one of those bench names wasn't happy, our team was ready to act and start the interview process quickly.

One of my favorite examples of success from the bench was a young man working as an engineer in a separate niche. He was good friends with one of our team members, so she asked us to add him to the bench. We brought him in for an initial interview and agreed that he seemed like a great fit for our team; however, at the time, we were not hiring, and the budget was really tight that year, so he remained on the bench for seven more months. As soon as we were looking to hire again, we reached out to him and continued the interview process. I'm happy to say he is still a pivotal member of the team today.

Rockstar Hires

Whether from The Bench, networking events, or standard hiring processes, we've been blessed to have some extraordinary team members over the years. The value they brought to the company is immeasurable.

Matt

Over the course of several years, we added many really great rockstars to our team. One of the first was Matt, an architect from our niche with tremendous attention to detail, a love of his craft, and a passion for teaching others, all of which we desperately needed in our growing organization. Matt quickly became a vital component of our leadership team. Where I enjoy moving fast and sometimes breaking things, Matt prefers thorough due diligence up front and attempting to modify without breaking—a complementary skill that all leadership teams should have.

A fun life lesson that I try to remember is actually how we recruited Matt. A few members of our team were attending an industry golf outing. While Matt wasn't there, the owner of the firm he worked for was. One of the guys on my team accidentally hit a golf ball near the group in front of us, which happens frequently on the golf course, especially in large group events. As our guys approached the group while apologizing and retrieving their ball, one member of that group began yelling and acting less than professional. That was the end of that incident until dinner later that evening, where one of our guys was talking to an industry friend about what had occurred. The industry friend said, "Oh, don't worry about that guy. He's a Jerk. But I really should introduce you to Matt. He's a great guy who works for him and deserves better; you'll love him." We quickly contacted Matt and interviewed him. Our industry friend was right. We did love him.

Joe

Later that same year, we hired another absolute rockstar named Joe. Joe did not have an engineering degree and was not working for an engineering firm. He was working on the construction side of the industry, performing the physical labor for projects similar to those that we designed. From the first interview, it was clear that Joe was a fantastic guy who was a tremendous fit for our core values. Our concern, though, was a lack of formal engineering experience. We knew he understood the work to be performed likely better than most of us, but would he be able to perform the other duties required? Our gut told us that he would, but we decided to give him a small project to verify. During the interview process we asked him to take a look at a building that we had recently performed an investigation on and write a brief report of the conditions he identified and how he proposed addressing those issues. Ultimately, we really wanted to see if he was willing to put this relatively small investment of time in and if he was willing to be vulnerable enough to put himself out there by performing a new task and then submitting that for review.

Well, Joe crushed it. In addition to providing the report earlier than expected, it was more comprehensive and accurate than we anticipated. That was a foretelling of Joe's natural wiring. He consistently over-delivered and did so with an immense amount of humility. I am incredibly grateful we gave Joe that assignment; otherwise, we may not have "taken a chance" on him. What a miss that would've been.

Tom

At the same time that we were hiring Joe, we were looking for a Business Development Associate. This was not a common position in our niche, so we knew we needed to find someone outside. However, we anticipated finding someone used to selling engineering services or, at minimum, professional services B2B (Business to Business) in New York City. Tom, the best candidate we interviewed from a core values perspective, had been selling B2C (Business to Consumer) in southern New Jersey.

Like we had done with Joe, we decided to give Tom an assignment. Our gatekeeper, Donna, was one of the most stringent in the industry at preventing sales calls from coming through and interrupting my day. So, we gave Tom the assignment of coming up with an alias and attempting to get past Donna and through to me. If he reached me, we would know that he had potential. Not only did Tom make it past Donna with flying colors, but he had me hook, line, and sinker. I was fully bought into the persona he played. We still laugh at how much I fell for it when the assignment was partly my idea.

Within a few months, Tom was crushing it and beloved by our team and our clients alike. Again, it was laughable that we even considered passing on him for not having the exact experience we were looking for. Thank God we decided to give Tom this assignment, verifying what our gut was telling us.

Will your recruiting and hiring process allow you to find rockstars? What can you do to improve it?

Patricia

As we grew, we certainly experienced the philosophy taught in Marshall Goldsmith's book, *What Got You Here Won't Get You There*. What we looked for in team members and clients evolved.

When we were a scrappy startup, we landed some clients because we were inexpensive and/or because I, the owner, was intimately involved in every project, and for some clients, that was important. As we grew, however, I could not be involved with every aspect of every project, and we increased our fees to catch up to the industry. We contemplated developing several tiers of product offerings and pricing similar to the Honda-Acura-Lexus model but, ultimately, decided that wasn't right for us, so we had to move away from those clients. Because they were good clients to us all along, we didn't want to completely abandon them, so we introduced them to industry friends who had more recently started their own firms and were happy to serve them much like we had when we started out.

Similarly, some of our team members were not willing or able to keep up with the growth of the firm, so we had to allow them to find work that they would love elsewhere. This was a much harder realization to come to grips with as we loved our team, so seeing people who were good people and at one time were great fits for their roles leave the company was a challenge. We needed to realize, though, that not everyone wants to grow and be involved in growing organizations, or perhaps just not at the rapid pace that we were growing, and there's nothing wrong with that. We had several great people leave, by our decision or theirs, who ended up in organizations growing at a pace they are much more comfortable with. In fact, one former team member started his own firm, and two former team members joined him. It's a great feeling knowing that we played a part in them connecting, and they found more comfort in the new firm's growth rate.

From an overall business perspective, the mantra of "what got you here won't get you there" also relates to the expansion of new roles that didn't previously exist. When I started the business, I was our bookkeeper and was so for much longer than I should've been. I created invoices, followed up on AR, and paid bills mostly on weekends. When I finally realized that process couldn't continue, we hired a controller. We were blessed to find Patricia. She was fantastic, overqualified, for sure, but willing to take the role as it was close to home, and she was re-entering the working world after having been home with her young boys. She immediately saved us money on bills going out the door as well as catching fees on invoices that I had been missing or, for insecure reasons, just wasn't charging to clients. As we continued to grow, though, the time required for the role quickly became more than we had discussed and required more time than Patricia wanted to put in while being available for her young boys. Fortunately, she gave us plenty of notice to help us find our next finance guru, another benefit of hiring really good people.

Josh

By this point, we were getting more confident in our ambitious growth projections, so we decided to look for someone with the capabilities to be our controller now but also be the CFO we would need in just a few short years. We interviewed several great candidates but chose Josh. I almost missed out on hiring Josh because of the way we found him. I received a LinkedIn message from a new connection, Joey, who I didn't know, with Josh's resume and heaping praise on him. My skeptical mind thought, *Who does that? Who is that nice that they connect someone they don't know with a potential great hire?* Ultimately, I realized that Joey could just be that thoughtful and helpful, so we should at least have Josh come in for a first interview. Again, it's laughable that I almost missed out on Josh because I was concerned someone was being too nice. As it turns out, not only did Josh become a pivotal member of our leadership team and a great friend, but Joey became a good friend as well.

Josh's experience and financial expertise were pivotal in helping us continue to grow and expand. He helped us focus more on profit and cash management while ensuring that our Accounts Receivable, Accounts Payable, and bookkeeping processes matured to the standard that a business of our size needed. In addition to being attuned to the business's financial success, Josh also ensured that I became more focused on my family's financial success.

When we started the business, like many entrepreneurs, we paid all bills every month, and what was left over at the end of the month, if anything, was the profit that came home. We eventually developed a better budgeting process, but if we missed our revenue numbers, then we'd miss profit, and we brought nothing home.

It wasn't until Josh incorporated the concepts of Michael Michalowicz's book, *Profit First*, that we really ratcheted up our focus on profit. The concepts in *Profit First* by no means condone not paying vendors or any other bills; it simply has you laser-focused on staying within budget. Psychologically, I was okay with going over budget if I was going to lose out on my own personal gain via profit, but I was not okay with going over budget if it meant not paying a vendor on time. It's a strange mindset to admit to, but apparently not that uncommon.

Who is your Josh?
Who is your finance guru? Who will you lean on for advice? Who will hold you accountable to ensure that you, the owner, are prioritizing your finances so that your budget includes all required expenses, including properly compensating yourself?

Jess

Another one of the many self-limiting beliefs I had to get past was that I didn't need, wasn't worthy of, and couldn't justify an executive assistant. When I finally decided to hire one, I didn't fully release my internal narrative of not being "worthy," so I started with a small mindset and decided to hire part-time at below what the market would pay for a role. As such, I was only able to recruit candidates who had never performed the role and weren't truly passionate about being an EA. However, even with some struggles in hiring the right EA, my eyes were opened to the impact that the right one would have on our entire business and me personally.

So, after four failed attempts at hiring the right EA, we hired Jess—she was a godsend. In addition to being a great core value fit, incredibly smart, and dedicated, she is also very passionate about the role of an EA. Jess was always happiest when she could set me up to have a great day accomplishing the tasks that only I could or should do and delegating the remaining tasks to others. Using delegation filters to communicate my desired outcome, I was able to give complete control of my calendar, email, scheduling new business meetings, most communication, and many other critical tasks that I didn't enjoy and that she was much better at. Jess embraced them all wholeheartedly.

One interesting psychological head game we realized was that I found networking events, new business meetings, and conferences to be fun, so I often felt guilty going to them and felt like I should be doing something else. Subconsciously, then, I had a tendency not to make them a priority when making my schedule. Of course, I knew deep down that it was in the best interest of the business for me to do those things, but for some reason, I still hesitated. We decided that the number of those meetings I had would be one of Jess's measurables. She was responsible for scheduling the meetings, and it was something she would be evaluated on, meaning that if I didn't hit those numbers, Jess would be penalized. Once I knew that Jess would be financially penalized by not making her bonus if I didn't make the meetings a priority, it was a totally different level of accountability. Jess would schedule the meetings, and I would never come up with something more important.

In full disclosure, this didn't happen immediately and wasn't fully my idea. It came up in a discussion that Jess and I had after we had worked together for some time, and there was a professional level of comfort that she knew I wouldn't miss the goal if it meant her individual gain.

Additionally, we implemented the concept of The Front Stage/Back Stage Model® from Strategic Coach. As the name implies, it adapts the theater mindset for business where there is an entire team backstage focused purely on the success of those that are "Front Stage." The production isn't going to be a success without both teams playing their part and recognizing that both parts are equally important. Jess did all the work of prepping me for my new business meetings, networking events, and internal meetings, so I just had to show up and handle the part I loved.

On some of the days that I had the most success and the most fun, I would have four or five client and networking meetings in a day. We would spend 20 minutes discussing the schedule several days in advance, reviewing who I was going to meet, any projects or opportunities to discuss, and any feedback that she obtained from our team that they wanted me to address or be aware of. As I approached each meeting Jess would send me a text with bullet points of everything I needed to know for the meeting and the questions that I might want to ask. An hour later, as I left that meeting, I would text her with my notes and she would send me back the bullet points for the next one that I was running to. If I was heading to a networking event, she would comb through the attendance list and let me know who would be there that I wanted to meet. This made my day so seamless and incredibly productive. Once I sent the notes from the first meeting to Jess, I could free my mind to focus on the next meeting and so on.

The next morning, Jess would have drafts of thank you emails ready for me to send to everyone I met and summaries of any follow-up items. I could likely spend a whole chapter on the value that a great Executive Assistant brought to my business and me personally, but I'll stop here. I'll just simply state that when mentoring a new entrepreneur recently and he asked who his first hire should be, without hesitation, I said a great EA. Similar to me in the early days, he is a solopreneur with a consulting firm, so essentially, he is his business right now. In my opinion, he can easily double his productivity and revenue with a Jess.

As we all know, we make plans, and God laughs. I was adamant that I needed an Executive Assistant who was in the office full time, so I would not even consider someone working from home full time. Well, we hired Jess full-time in January 2020, and two months later, she, like all of us, was working full-time from home. She absolutely crushed it working from home and completely changed my mindset. The right EA in the right situation can absolutely be a rockstar from home or anywhere.

Do you have an Executive Assistant? If not, go out and find yourself a Jess, and please don't wait as long as I did.

Connecting Good People

Our focus wasn't strictly on bringing rockstars into the team, we truly did a great job of surrounding ourselves with really good people outside the organization as well. I've always felt fulfilled when

I've connected good people from different circles. So, while reading Keith Ferrazzi's book *Never Eat Alone*, I decided to adopt one of his great ideas for my own use.

Keith has some great strategies for networking and building stronger professional networks, but what really hooked me were the events he hosted at his home. He described hosting events at his apartment in Los Angeles for seemingly random groups of friends and colleagues, allowing them to connect. Keith would invite ten or so people and an "anchor tenant." The intent of the anchor tenant was simply to have someone at the party that he knew his network would love to meet but was currently outside of their social circle—someone who could "add a little electricity." Keith had no expectations of a direct return for himself; he just wanted to bring value to his network.[8] I loved that idea, but Mary Jo wasn't likely going to be cool with me inviting a dozen people to our three-bedroom suburban colonial. If she did agree to this idea, in reality, who would come?

I modified Keith's idea and called it Lunch at the Vault. I felt more comfortable hosting small groups, and so did our budget, so I started hosting monthly events of ten people. We would meet at a steakhouse in the Wall Street area for lunch on Fridays that would often spill into cocktails afterward and bleed into the evening. I would invite one or two people from each of my different Centers of Influence lists: clients, industry friends, Manhattan College alumni, family/friends, executives association, and a few others. Occasionally, I would also encourage guests to invite one of their Centers of Influence. I didn't deliberately invite "anchor tenants," but from time to time, we ended up with one.

The goal, as I said at the start of every lunch, was just to connect good people. We all deal with challenging people on a regular basis. I felt very blessed to also deal with some really good people. So, why shouldn't I make an effort to connect those good people to each other, and maybe, eventually, we could all surround ourselves with more and more good people? The steakhouse was in an old bank building that had a vault in the basement. Initially I just thought the space was very private and very, very cool. But the best part turned out to be that we had no phone service down there, so we were completely present the entire time. We would talk about our personal and professional aspirations and connect deeper. Of course, we had a great time and tons of laughs as well.

At one of the more memorable lunches, I invited Dennis, a lifelong friend from childhood, and Sean, a friend from a networking group. Sean invited Paula, a neighbor of his and a potentially huge client. When I learned Paula was coming, I panicked. In addition to Dennis, I had another longtime friend coming as well. The thought of Paula being in the same room as two guys that I crushed underage beers with back in the day was horrifying. Well, as it turned out, we'd all grown up, at least a little anyway, and the lunch was one of the best. Dennis and Paula knew many of the same people, and we were all engrossed in their stories.

I truly love connecting good people, and it has been incredibly rewarding to watch some of the relationships that started at our Lunch at the Vault events turn into long-term friendships, business relationships, or mentorships.

Are you comfortable networking in large group settings or small ones? What types of events do you enjoy attending that you could consider replicating for your network? What can you do to add value to your network with no expectations of a return?

Sustainable Growth Rate

Our business had a solid footing. We were growing, connecting, and trying to do all the right things to continue to be successful. Then, in 2016, I learned about the term sustainable growth rate . . . the hard way. In early April of that year, my accountant informed me of a very large tax bill that I had due April 15th. I had less than a week to come up with approximately $200,000 to pay the IRS. Because of the speed at which we were growing, I didn't pay much attention to our profit on paper; I paid more attention to the cash flow in the door. I also didn't proactively reach out to our accountant, and he didn't proactively reach out to me—that's a bad combination. Finding out, roughly six days before tax day, that I owed the IRS approximately $200,000 and had nowhere near that in my personal and professional bank account was not a fun experience. Things got very real for me, and I laid awake every night, terrified that I was going to lose the house, the business, everything.

Well, as it turned out, the IRS was actually pretty reasonable to deal with as long as I proactively approached them, explained the situation, and worked out a payment plan. From what I understand, they're relatively reasonable to work with once, but if I had done it again, they likely wouldn't have been so understanding. Also, since I had a reasonable plan that showed them how I was going to pay it back within six months, they were fairly sympathetic. At least, that was my experience. I made sure that every month, I had at least, if not more, than the payment we had agreed to. We paid off the debt to the IRS early and made sure we had our future payments lined up every single quarter from there moving forward to avoid any future April surprises.

I am not by any stretch encouraging anyone to delay paying their taxes on purpose. Learn from my mistake; trust me when I say the stress was not worth it. I share this story because things come up as an entrepreneur that you think will destroy your business and your family. But if you take some time to speak to some good advisors, take a few deep breaths, and set up a good plan to resolve it, you can and will get through it.

You'll also learn the lesson to make sure you never make that mistake again. As you start your business, line yourself up with a really good accountant, and do not wait for them to reach out to you. Be very proactive with them. I promise you never want to go home and tell your spouse you have this massive debt to the IRS because you had your head in the sand. We both laid awake for many nights in April, May, and June that year.

So, where does the term sustainable growth rate come in? Based on the seasonality of our business, our revenue and profit peaked in the summer and were lowest in the winter every year. Our philosophy was to keep the profit in the business to reinvest in continued growth, so we often saw our cash balances get frighteningly low in March and April. As we grew each year, we were hiring people in the winter to have them onboard, trained, and ready for the following spring and summer. This obviously ate into the previous year's profit.

I've seen several detailed formulas on how to accurately calculate the sustainable growth rate, but from what I've learned, a good rule of thumb is 2:1 growth to profit. We had several strong years of growth; however, this particular year, revenue growth was 39 percent. So, with an annual profit rate of 15 percent, it was clear why we ran into cash issues. So, we had two choices: reduce future growth rates to less than 30 percent or increase profit.

With a business purpose to empower others to improve their quality of life, we knew that focusing on increasing profit was the obvious choice. Reducing growth goals would reduce the impact that we would have.

Recognition

The result of not reducing growth goals was that we were named to the Inc. 5000 list of fastest-growing privately held companies in the US from 2017–2021. Truthfully, it's the fastest-growing companies that *applied* for the Inc. 5000, but that's neither here nor there; we made it to the list. We had been named to several other lists for growth as well but none as widely recognized as Inc's. Many people view these types of awards and accolades as a vanity exercise, and there is some degree of truth to that. However, it's important to note that competitive teams like winning and recognition of business awards feel like winning. Whether the award is for the fastest growth, client satisfaction, best firms to work for, etc., all provide an opportunity for team members to give each other a pat on the back. Perhaps more importantly though, the application process gives a chance to be very introspective into what the team is doing well and what areas we can work on.

For example, the Zweig Best Firms to Work For award, given by an engineering management consulting group, provided all applicants with the curated survey results of all other companies that applied. This allows each firm to learn from the others where they were strong and where they could improve. Just by having our team fill out the survey, we learned some great feedback that they had not shared with leadership.

Brand awareness is another benefit of award recognition. Using the awards for marketing purposes helped us from a business development perspective as well as with recruitment; everyone wants to be associated with "winning" teams. Taking this point to another level, the firm that ultimately acquired our engineering firm initially found us on the Inc. 5000 list.

These awards often are coupled with conferences, some of which can bring great networking and new valuable resources. At one of these events, I attended a breakout session by an expert in small business funding strategies, Ami Kassar, who has become a trusted resource for me and several friends. At another breakout session, I met a tax strategist specializing in the engineering space, Dawson Fercho, whose wisdom and guidance have benefitted me to the tune of a half-million dollars. I also met Pete Atherton, author of *Reversing Burnout*, at one of these conferences. His consulting services are helping to solve the growing concern of leadership burnout in the engineering industry.

Initially, I was hesitant to apply for awards as it felt purely ego-driven, but the value that the recognition and the award process itself brings for the right awards was well worth it. The lessons learned, the advice received, the contacts made, and the rare opportunity to stand up tall and share that victory with the team brought great value to us all.

Dear Brian,

In 2018, you were named one of Inc. 5000's Honorees. Myself and the kids were so excited for you and beyond proud. The convention and gala were being held at a beautiful resort in San Antonio, Texas, and you thought it would be great to celebrate this amazing accomplishment with the kids. You said that you wanted to show your gratitude to them for all the sacrifices they made while you started and ran the business. This is a phrase you often used with them and still do: "All of the sacrifices they made while you ran the business." I love the puzzled little faces I would see when you said this to them. They had no idea what you meant or what they had sacrificed, but they knew they felt special when you said it. They felt a part of what you were creating. You headed out to Texas a few days earlier than me and the kids to attend some of the events and hear some of the amazing speakers they had lined up.

We arrived at Newark Airport, myself and the five kids, and the security line was like nothing I'd ever seen before. Gavin looked at me, and I tried to put on a brave face. The kids grew more and more concerned the longer we waited on the line; I was internally panicking. How could I call you and tell you we missed our flight? How could I have failed you at this momentous time in your career? Just as the six of us made it through security, we could hear the overhead announcement for the last call for our flight to San Antonio, Texas. I looked at Gavin, who was twelve at the time, and said, "Run." He didn't say a word. He grabbed Dolan's hand and took off. The girls were behind him, and I was pushing Finn in the carriage behind them. I remember Julia started crying, and Adanya told her we were going to make it. Gavin had gotten so far ahead that I could no longer see him and Dolan. Over the years, with Finn's medical woes, Padre Pio had become my go-to Saint. I was running through the terminal, just saying out loud, "Please, Padre Pio. Please, Padre Pio." By the time I made it to the gate, the attendant was standing there with the other four children and said, "We were just closing the door, and your son yelled, 'Stop, please.'" The six of us boarded the plane, and we took off within minutes. I looked at Gavin and mouthed, "Thank you," and he gave his classic reply, "No sweat, Mom." I thanked Jesus; he is so much like you!

You and I have talked frequently about how that trip to San Antonio was sort of the line in the sand for the business and our family. Things were different after that trip, and different in a good way. After eight years of burdening all this stress on your shoulders, you could finally exhale. It was kind of your "I made it" moment. I could not have been more proud of you that evening, babe.

I love you,
MJ

Birthing of Giants

At one of the Inc. 5000 conferences, I had the pleasure of hearing Lewis Schiff speak. Lewis is the Chairman of the Board of the Birthing of Giants Fellowship program, in addition to being the author of *The First Habit* and leader of several other entrepreneurial mentorship and education initiatives. That conference and introduction led to me attending a weeklong Birthing of Giants fellowship program on the campus of Duke University in Durham, North Carolina, in April 2019. Spending the better part of a week with fellow entrepreneurs whose ambitions of building and growing their companies was enticing, but what really made the program so impactful was the focus on building a great company that serves their team and their clients, not just themselves.

As part of the program, we walked through a "Built to Sell" roadmap. Although many of us didn't intend to sell our business at that time, many of the steps necessary to prepare for a sale are beneficial for most businesses, so the exercise was incredibly productive for all of us. Two other great aspects of the program were identifying the biggest opportunity lurking within our company and determining what we wanted our company to look like next year and in five years.

Of course, any thorough business program will incorporate business development, so we did a rather deep dive into sales management, our brand, and our network. We examined what our sales management looks like in our organization versus what it should look like. Next, we examined our network, one of my favorite topics, as well as how to upgrade our network. I came away from the review of my network, realizing that I needed to be more intentional in identifying people who *use their faith to run their business, someone who's written a book, and someone who's sold a portion of their business.* Clearly, the wheels were starting to turn back then for this next chapter.

Using the concepts in his book, Lewis helped us define our language, or how we interact with the world, and then analyze how we actually spend our day and whether it engaged or exhausted us.

At the end of the week, Lewis had us set a One Year From Today (OYFT) goal. After diving into the business for four days, I set a goal to have "Management Team 1.5" in place within the year. I added the follow-up statement, "We have a strong L/T that is good at setting goals and works really hard. We are just inexperienced and don't have enough accountability and conflict." In addition to the OYFT goal, I also recognized the urgent need to focus on growing profit, which, thank God, I did, as you'll see when COVID-19 hit.

Do you know what your One Year From Today goal is?
Do you need the help of other business leaders to help you clarify or strengthen it?

Harvard Business School

One of the hurdles I felt I struggled with as an entrepreneur was a lack of a formal business education. As the company grew, I projected that this would become a bigger and bigger issue, so I began looking into several MBA and Executive MBA programs. After narrowing down my list, I spoke to Mark, our EOS Implementer, and he quickly and thankfully gave me a different perspective. He asked if I wanted to sit in all of the classes required to get a traditional MBA. I thought for a minute and said no, I really just wanted to learn more about some aspects. After further discussion, Mark pointed out that, at this point in my entrepreneurial journey, I didn't need to get an MBA; I needed to hire an MBA. Well, that was a much more attractive alternative. Mark is a big advocate for continuing education, so he wasn't trying to talk me out of a program altogether but rather wanted to make sure I invested my time and money into the right one. He recommended Harvard Business School's Owner/President Management (OPM) program. After researching that program and several other advanced education programs for business owners, I knew that Mark was right; OPM was the program for me. So, in 2019, I attended the first of three 3-week units on the HBS campus.

Surrounded by incredibly accomplished entrepreneurs and leaders from around the world, I quickly realized the benefit of attending a high-commitment program at an elite institution. From the opening session through the last class, the quality of the education and, even more so, the ability of the incredible faculty resulted in a top-notch education, much of which I am still processing.

The program was intense and packed a significant educational experience in three different three-week-long sprints. This was my first experience with the case study method; reviewing real-world business examples brought tremendous value. This was then amplified by the discussion that ensued with the room full of incredibly talented business owners from around the world facilitated by the world-class faculty. We spent a total of nine weeks on campus reviewing cases on topics such as leadership, finance, negotiations, strategy, and innovation, as well as others.

Outside the classroom, we had some great discussions about business, family, and faith. We learned so much about each other, about our cultures, and about our different viewpoints on past and current political, social, and business issues. I created some incredibly strong friendships with truly remarkable people that I'm confident will last a lifetime.

To be completely honest, what surprised me most about the program, though, was the willingness of all to openly discuss faith, ethics, and morals. It was really a great group of people, students and faculty alike. Some of my biggest takeaways had nothing to do with finance, marketing, or any other typical business theme for that matter; they had to do with the emphasis on being good, decent leaders and assisting others. As stated by Professor Ananth Raman, We have an obligation to enable others to take their shot.

I graduated from the program in early 2023 and came away with an amplified feeling that I had experienced at the Inc. 5000 conferences, Strategic Coach sessions, and the Executives Association in New York City. Most business owners that I've interacted with are good, decent people who genuinely care for their team, want to succeed to provide for their family, care about providing a great product, and are rooting for each other, not against each other. As reflected by HBS's first mission statement, its purpose is to educate leaders to "make a decent profit—decently."[9]

Dear Brian,

We left for Port-Au-Prince, Haiti, the day after Easter Sunday, 2019. We were in the midst of adopting Grace, and the time had come to spend the mandatory two weeks in Haiti with her in order to complete our socialization visit. The flight down was such an internal roller coaster: leaving behind the other five kids, split between your parents and my mom, leaving behind your now fast-paced growing business, and meeting Grace for the first time. On top of all of that, knowing we were going to have to leave her there in Haiti after the two weeks was just gnawing away at my insides. You held my hand for most of the entire flight.

When we touched down in Port-Au-Prince, and the doors of the airplane opened, the smells and sounds of the city wrapped around me like a warm, cozy blanket on a winter night. It had been 23 years since I last set foot in Haiti. Haiti is one of those countries that, once you've been blessed to visit, it leaves a permanent indentation on your heart. You're changed forever and for the better; the way you look at the world and your view of people is never the same. This particular Monday in 2019 was like a dream come true. I was standing there in the Port-Au-Prince airport holding your hand, getting to share this amazing country with you, this country that had lassoed my heart over 20 years prior. Getting to meet our beautiful daughter for the first time was the cherry on top.

We took the long, winding road up to the Kenscoff Mountains, where Grace's creche was located. The ride up was so surreal; I was just full of so much gratitude to you and our Lord. It had only been a little over three years since we brought Finn home from China, and here we were in Haiti, about to meet and hold our daughter Grace. So many of the same emotions that filled us in Beijing when we met Finn for the first time were beginning to resurface.

We quickly dropped our bags off at the house we would be staying at for the two weeks and continued the rest of the way to the orphanage by foot down a dirt road. I remember walking through the gates of the creche with you and being greeted by about five little friendly faces. We were escorted into a little room, all four walls lined with cribs. Grace was all of three years old at the time, and my eye caught her standing next to her crib, holding onto it, wearing a little denim skirt and cream sweatshirt, just staring at us as we walked in. You knelt down on one knee, and one of the nannies directed Gracie to go over to you. She slowly walked over to you, you scooped her up, and she began to run her hand along the scruff of your beard. She just stared at you while her little hand ran up and down the side of your cheek. I felt this immense rush of love for God giving us this gift of Grace, for you and your heart and your love for our little Gracie.

We spent the next two weeks at the creche from morning to night. We were there each morning when Grace was waking up, and we put her into bed each evening before heading back to the house. We spent the days playing with the kids and helping out with the feedings and changes of all the little ones. Grace had started to bond with both of us, and we were so enjoying our time there with her. We would FaceTime the kids back at home during the day so they would get to spend some time with her as well; it was so hard being apart from each other, but we were all brave, remembering this was only temporary.

After leaving the creche each night, we'd recap our day to each other, cracking up at the times Grace made us laugh. It only took a day or two for her larger-than-life sense of humor to surface. Being at the creche every day for ten hours gave us the chance to not only bond with Grace but also to connect with so many of the children there. They all had such wonderful personalities, and all desired our attention and love. It was such a gift to be sharing this experience with you. Grace wiggled her way into our hearts, and leaving her there in Haiti at the end of those two weeks was, hands down, one of the worst days of our lives. But as in all things, we leaned on each other and our faith to give us the strength. I remember Tatito, Grace's favorite Nanny in the creche, who loved her just as much as I do, looking at me while tears were rolling down my face and saying in broken English, "Courage, Mama, courage." And for the next year, until Gracie was home with us, I kept putting myself back in that room, lined with all the cribs, and hearing Tatito tell me, "Courage, Mama, courage."

It was so nice to be back home and to see the other five kids again. You often refer to us as a wolf-pack; we're just better when we're all together. And that could not be more true! We spent the next few weeks at home sharing our stories with the kids and all of our family about our time at the creche with Grace. We spoke of so many of the kids we had met and connected with, but there was this one little young guy, slightly older than Dolan at the time, who had really caught our attention. "R" was bright-eyed and cautious, very intelligent and mature for his age. You and I found ourselves drawn to him, and, most days, he would sit with the two of us and Grace and share lunch with us. We told the kids all about him and how we should pray that he finds a family because he is such a special little boy. He would be a blessing to any family, we told them.

You and I had decided that knowing it was going to take another year before Grace's paperwork was processed and she could officially come home to us, you would take some in-between trips to visit her. We were so blessed that there was a direct flight from Newark, NJ, to Port-Au-Prince. In June 2019, you and Gavin took a long weekend down to Haiti to visit our Gracie girl. I had so much gratitude to you for going to see her and for loving on her for all of us. We all missed her, and it made me and the kids so happy to know that you and Gavin would be there for a few days with her. You FaceTimed us many times a day, and it was such a gift to get to see Grace and talk to her. It was amazing to see how she remembered you and was bonding with you. And to see Gavin with her was wonderful. Grace had climbed into Gavin's heart just like ours, and that was clear in all the pictures you were sending us. What was also becoming clear to both of us, without having to say it to each other, was that R was also making his way into our hearts. You sent one particular photo of Gavin with him that just made me think, Is God trying to tell us something?

You and Gavin flew back home on a Sunday, and I remember you and I stayed up chatting that night after all the kids went to bed. I asked you if you thought the reason why R hadn't found a family yet was because we were it. Your answer was, "I think you might be right." The next morning, I reached out to our adoption agency, HOLT, and we started the process of bringing home our son R that same week.

Four-plus long years after submitting our initial paperwork to adopt R, we were officially matched and got to see his beautiful face on Zoom the day after Thanksgiving, 2023. God is good. I can't say that over these past four years, you and I didn't exhibit large amounts of doubt toward a process that made it seem as if R would never come home to us. But, overall, we have the faith to know God is in control of R's journey as well as ours. And having that faith gave us the strength to endure the pain of being away from him for these past four years. We were both overjoyed on that Zoom call to tell R how much we love him and how hard we have tried over the past four years to bring him home. To hear him call you Papa and me, Mama made this a Thanksgiving neither one of us will ever forget. Please, God, let these next few steps go quickly over the next year so we can bring R home to join his "pack."

I love you,
MJ

Transparency Creates Opportunities

We had shared with the team early on that we wanted to expand our geographic footprint and regularly gave them the list of cities we were considering. Because we had created a culture where people could talk with us about their long-term plans, our team was comfortable approaching us to let us know when they had thoughts about moving out of the New York area. Sometimes, it was because they had family obligations that would take them to another city or because they would simply enjoy seeing other parts of the country. We had a pretty sizable list of team members on our team who were wanting, or at least willing, to move. Having this list benefitted us greatly when we started to grow and land some long-term projects in other states. So, when we landed a contract with a large national bank to work on hundreds of buildings throughout the U.S., we knew which team members to go to. As some of those West Coast projects became long-term opportunities, we had insight into the team members who would be willing to stay out west for a few months or even longer if needed.

Similarly, the culture we created with this type of transparency benefited us when we had team members who wanted to move to an area we weren't planning on serving soon. They knew that we would consider shifting their roles rather than seeing them leave the company. We adjusted to allow them to do that work remotely from places like Colorado, Las Vegas, and Arizona. Now, we had boots on the ground in those states should an opportunity arise, and those opportunities certainly did.

When an opportunity came up for a large client in Boston, one of my team members approached and said, "Hey, I've been thinking about moving to Boston. My wife's family is from up there. It would give us a chance to be closer to them, and it would give me a chance to see what it's like to launch an office." That conversation happened fairly quickly after we landed the opportunity to go to Boston because the seeds had been sown long before. We had been open about the conversations, sharing it with the team. And although, in some instances, the team didn't seem to react, they were thinking and praying about it at home and talking to their significant others. So when the actual opportunities arose, they had a head start and were ready for the transition.

As we started to grow our team, our projections of our growth showed we should look at opportunities outside of New York City. So, we started doing some research on all of the major geographic markets for our niche in the United States. That research included population growth, number of skyscrapers, large warehouses, types of clients, how many Fortune 500 companies were in the area, and various other objective data.

We also wanted subjective data, so we spoke to friends in the industry about each of the target markets. We had a list of over fifty different geographic markets and narrowed it down to about fifteen ideal ones. Then, we spoke to those friends who were familiar with the specific markets. We also spoke to clients and contractors in those markets and found out what they knew, what they thought of the market, and whether or not, from a client's perspective, they could benefit from us offering services in those markets. When we first started making these calls to our clients, I was nervous about what they would think of us just calling them up and saying, "Hey, we're looking at expanding into the Charlotte, North Carolina, region. Is that an area that you'd like us to service?" So, when we called the clients, we would give them a list of five of the target markets that were on our list of fifteen, especially if we knew they had facilities there. We were upfront and honest with them, explaining that we were looking to expand our geographic reach. We asked if it would benefit them if we expanded to any or all of these geographic markets.

The information we got from our clients was tremendous and incredibly valuable. Sure, there were a few who shut us down and said, "You're serving us in New York, and that's enough." But there were more who were excited at the prospect of having someone they enjoyed working with servicing them in other markets.

One of our largest clients was based out of Boston, Massachusetts. We were working for them on a few projects on some facilities they had in New York, but a bulk of their facilities were in New England and on the West Coast. They were a phenomenal client to deal with, from the type of portfolio they had as well as their payment terms, ease of working with, and, most of all, just the fact that they were good people. I didn't know their head of East Coast operations all that well, but I took a shot and reached out to him anyway. "Would you be willing to take some time to meet to discuss some target markets that we're looking into expanding into and see if we can help serve you in those markets?" I asked. He responded almost instantly. "Sure, absolutely. Would you be willing to come up here?" Naively, I thought he wanted me to come up to Boston to meet. But what he meant was, would we be willing to open an office in Boston. Now, the interesting thing was our data showed that the Boston Market was saturated with our competition.

We agreed to meet with them to talk about our team doing some work for them in Boston and opening an office. At the meeting, I shared that our data showed that Boston was saturated with competition, including many firms that had been around for decades. He responded with, "Yes, but they don't return phone calls. We need people who return our phone calls." It was as simple as that. Our team understood the value of returning phone calls because we focused not just on the technical but also the personal side of how to treat a client. And as a result, we landed a lot of work from this client. In a prime market, we opened an office and grew a team in the Boston area because we returned phone calls. Sounds simple, I know, but getting people to understand the value of picking up the phone, returning a phone call, and responding via email in a timely manner is becoming a lost art.

We likely picked up a million dollars worth of work from this client within the first year and a half of our team's presence in Boston simply because we returned phone calls. Yes, of course, the rest of our services were great, probably on par with the firms they were working with before, but our responsiveness set us apart.

Too Much Transparency?

In several iterations, we decided to up our marketing game, and in one of those, we invested in some video content. We wanted something that really highlighted the professionalism of our team and the quality of the services we provided, so we talked with a marketing team about what we were looking for. We explained that we wanted to show our clients and the industry in general that we are relatable and that we are human as well as professionals. The video team spent three days with us in the office and the field.

When the video production company was done with our film, they talked to our head of BD, Tom, and explained that they had a really good time shooting the video with our team. They said our team, especially our engineers, was a funny group that was very relatable and fun to hang out with. However, the video didn't relay that. Every time the camera went on, we were uptight, tense, and clenched. So, aside from the marketing video, they created a blooper video. Tom surprised our team with it at our annual retreat. It was hilarious. He proposed to our leadership team that we share this blooper video on social media and with our clients. As much as I love the video and embrace being vulnerable, that, for me, was a stretch. But thank God, I agreed.

Within the first week, the marketing video that we spent a lot of time on and our hard-earned dollars investing in had 5000 views. The blooper video, on the other hand, had over 10,000 views. That growth continued. For as long as I can recall, the blooper video always had many, many more views than the actual marketing video. This was great. It allowed people to see that we're vulnerable, we're human, and we openly acknowledge the fact that we're not perfect. And in certain ways, we could be fun to be around.

When it came to our presentations to our clients, though, I was still uncomfortable using the blooper video. Tom continued to encourage me to use it. I agreed, but when the time came for a meeting with a client, I would get nervous and not want to share the video. The prime example of my struggle was when we landed a meeting with one of our largest clients, the one from Boston that I referred to above. We prepped for the meeting with this client several times and had the blooper video lined up for the end of the presentation. We even had a little visual cue to indicate if I was comfortable with sharing the blooper video. As we got near the end of the meeting, which was going relatively well, I got nervous. I sent the cue to Tom not to share the video. And as he received the cue, he looked right back at me with a big smile on his face, and hit play on the video.

There was no turning back. The video was now playing for one of our largest professional clients. And they started roaring, laughing. They loved it. When the video ended, they were still laughing. The Director of East Coast Operations approached me and said, "I could definitely see myself hanging out with you guys. We need to work together more." Obviously, it wasn't just because of the blooper video, but the video did highlight how our teams would connect and work well together. From watching that video, he knew we weren't people who were going to lie to him or try to pretend like we were perfect. We were willing to be vulnerable and admit when we made mistakes. So much was said about the values, personalities, and integrity of our team just by airing that video. Sometimes, it's really beneficial to be vulnerable. And while I didn't want to normalize mistakes, we are all human and make them.

Are you comfortable being transparent with your team? With your clients? How transparent do you want to be?

Hey Mary Jo,

The many lessons learned during this adolescent phase for our business and our family are very complementary to what a child goes through. When our kids grew out of the toddler phase, it was time to send them off to school. As our business evolved, it was time for me to obtain a formal leadership education.

As the kids went off to school, they met new friends, similarly, you and I expanded our friend group with like-minded couples that helped us develop as better parents. The business, too, met new people who joined our team or our network and had an incredible lasting impact, much like the lifelong friends that Gavin met in pre-K.

Again, similar to the life of a toddler, the life of the family and the business were certainly hectic. Somehow, we made it work because we worked together. Although we didn't spend much time with each other, we certainly worked in unison and supported each other. Without recognizing it, we were growing closer to each other and stronger in our faith. After all, as Rabbi Daniel Lapin states, "Business is a spiritual endeavor, and it brings us closer to one another and closer to God."[10]

As parents and business owners during the toddler years, we have so much more control over what our kids and our employees can do and experience on a daily basis. As the kids, the family, and the business move into adolescence, so many of these experiences are outside of our line of sight and control. Placing our faith in God, in each other, as well as in the kids and the employees, is necessary for growth. All the while praying that we laid a strong enough foundation through our teachings and our examples in those incredibly formative toddler years.

As we stepped back as parents and business owners to allow for the growth of each, fortunately, God stepped in. Without the faith that He would, we likely would've been those helicopter parents staring through the window of the pre-K, I only did that once, and the business owner who restricts the growth of the business.

Love,
Brian

V
EMERGING ADULTHOOD

The child grew and became strong, filled with wisdom,
and the favor of God was upon him.

—Luke 2:40

Our children grow up fast. In what feels like a blink of an eye, the precious baby we cradled in our arms is getting their driver's license and applying to colleges. Running a business can feel similar. There's a subtle transition from struggling to get employees, clients, and positive financial growth to reaching a pinnacle where everything is running smoothly. For many entrepreneurs, this is when the "itch" kicks in, and thoughts of "What's next" start surfacing.

At some point in any business owner's journey, they have to acknowledge the passing of the torch. Whether it is an entrepreneur moving on or a business owner retiring, many questions arise: *Have I accomplished everything I wanted to with this venture? What's next for the business? Where do I want it to go? What's next for me? Where do I want to go? If I move on, will the company thrive without me?*

Dear Brian,

The world has no shortage of COVID stories. At a time of panic and impending dread that overtook the world, there were glimmers of hope and God's radiant love trying to shine through the darkness. It was mid-March when the shutdowns started. You carried the folding table we had used for all of our family parties up from the basement into our bedroom, where you set up your make-shift office. Your phone went non-stop. Everyone, including your leadership team, was looking for you to have all the answers. All I heard over and over again from everyone who called you was, "What are you going to do?" It wasn't only from your business team; it was from friends of yours who also owned their own businesses. Everyone looked for you to lead them, to burden their fears with them, and have all the answers for them. At all times, you remained calm and steadfast. You assured your entire team that their safety and their family's safety were of your utmost concern and priority. You took every call and spent countless hours talking to anyone who needed to hear you and ask you questions. You shared your plans, your managing tactics, and processes during the pandemic with anyone who needed to hear it or could benefit from utilizing the same plan.

I witnessed you grow this company into something so special over the past almost ten years at the time. You were a born leader. I knew that, and your parents and two sisters knew that too. The success of the business came as no shock; you were in your lane, doing what you were born to do: lead. But witnessing you navigate this pandemic and carry the burden of so many people's fears on your shoulders, including our own, gave me an entirely different level of admiration and love for you.

We were in the process of adopting our daughter Grace at the time from Haiti. During this same time in mid-March, Grace's adoption paperwork and process were coming to its conclusion, and we were weeks away from being able to bring her home to us. The director of our process had informed us that Grace's passport was completed and relinquished, we were just awaiting one other piece of authentic paperwork from the Haitian Government declaring Grace officially ours. Under normal circumstances, this news would have been elating, but we were also informed that Haiti would be closing its borders to all outgoing flights within days due to the pandemic. They had already discontinued all incoming commercial flights into Haiti. The only flight operations were for American citizens wishing to leave Haiti before all outgoing flights were suspended for an infinite time. HOLT adoption agency's staff in Haiti was working on overdrive trying to get Grace's final piece of paperwork so she could board one of the final flights departing Haiti prior to the shutdown. Grace was born HIV positive with a heart condition of unknown prognosis at the time. The possibility of Grace remaining in Haiti during the pandemic had become an emergent priority. Brian spent his days on the phone with the business team members and his nights with me, trying to utilize every resource in our power to bring our baby girl home to us. The HOLT staff had put us in contact with a missionary couple, Grace's guardian angels to this day, Jeff and Teressa Ballard. I remember emailing Jeff and asking him if, by some small miracle, we were able to secure this last piece of paperwork for Grace and get her on their flight departing Port-au-Prince that next morning, would they be so kind as to escort her to Miami, where Brian would be waiting for her? I reiterated to Jeff in my email that it was going to take an absolute miracle to pull this off and get her on their flight. I remember Jeff's response back to me; it's ingrained in my head forever. It read, "Well, it's a good thing we have a God of miracles. Yes, of course, we will escort Grace on the flight to Brian."

You walked out our back door with your duffle bag in your hand and the fear in both our eyes was unparalleled. You had to depart for JFK that morning before we even knew if Grace's paperwork would be completed and she would be on that last flight with the Ballard's to Miami. Neither of us could bear to think of the "what ifs" if Grace didn't get on that flight. The kids and I were huddled around my phone in the kitchen, waiting to hear from Amanda from HOLT. My Mom was downstairs pacing, saying the rosary. You FaceTimed us from JFK airport once you got there. The airport terminal was completely empty, other than a handful of staff members, and you were preparing to board the plane when Amanda called us. They had gotten the paperwork and Grace was on her way to the airport to meet the Ballard's to fly to Miami. All I thought was Thank you, Lord. You are a God of miracles, for sure. Myself and the kids were in tears, jumping up and down with joy. Grace was coming home. You flew to Miami, met the Ballard's there in the Miami Airport and Grace was officially ours. You flew home the next morning to New Jersey with our baby girl. Out of the darkness, God gives light. During this time of overwhelming stress coming at you, Brian, from every direction, family, work, and the state of the world, you remain my rock, my gift.

I adore you!
MJ

COVID-19

From the start of the business, we often discussed and prepared for "emergencies." We talked openly about our "hit by a bus" plan, which was the plan for what would happen if I was hit by a bus. I'm not a morbid person, but I felt it was important for my team members and my family to have a plan in place for the business to succeed if I suddenly were not available. To be fair, the plan wasn't as thorough as it could've been, but it was a plan, and thankfully, we never needed it.

We also often planned for emergency weather days, most commonly snow days. After each snow day, we would assess what went well and what didn't and adjust the process from there. As a result, we ended up working through some extended weather interruptions from hurricanes, etc, progressively more seamlessly, but each time, reviewing and adjusting for the next time.

Throughout my career, I was often internally conflicted by reporting to an office during a snowstorm. Obviously, work must go on, but what I observed is that team members would often arrive at the office anytime between 8:00 am and 11:00, and each time someone walked in, half the office gathered around to hear their story of shoveling their car out of the snow, the traffic they sat in, the cars they saw stuck in the snow, etc. Finally, around lunchtime, people would settle in and start getting some work done, and by 2:30 or 3:00, people started leaving to make their trek home. Those who arrived at 8:00 and left at 5:00 resented those who arrived late and left early. Those who arrived at 11:00 and left at 2:30 had their own complaints. It was typically a counter-productive day. Wouldn't we all have been more productive if we had just worked from home?

So, when I started the business, we had the mindset that it didn't make sense to force our team to come into the office in the snow. Instead, we would ask everyone to be prepared to work from home whenever snow storms were predicted. We set up a cloud-based server early on for this reason, as well as for anticipated future expansion into multiple offices. We would share with our team that we valued their time; it didn't make sense to commute 5–6 hours to an office to work 2. We also encouraged them to seize the opportunity and enjoy the day somewhat. Save the time and hassle of commuting, get some work done from home, and sprinkle in some fun. We felt that if we could average six hours from each team member on a snow day, we were ahead of the game. So, we encouraged the team to take an extended break and go play with their kids, enjoy watching the snow, or do whatever would make the day more enjoyable.

This was under the mutual understanding that we didn't have team members taking advantage of the professional respect and courtesy. Occasionally, we would have someone who "forgot" to prepare for the snow day despite multiple reminders. As such, in those circumstances, this was treated as a sick day as they didn't "show up" to work.

These repeated reps resulted in increased productivity during storms, as well as an increase in appreciation in both directions between leadership and the team. However, the real fruit of the many reps of these storms and subsequent review of what worked and didn't was a well-vetted emergency preparedness plan that developed over the years.

So when the COVID-19 pandemic shut down the U.S. in March 2020, we were well prepared. Instead of having to develop a remote work plan, we were able to simply tweak the plan that we had put in place over the past ten years. Tom, one of our rockstar leaders, shared his concern for the pandemic at our quarterly meeting in February. I'm embarrassed to say that we dismissed it initially, even laughing it off at first. However, Tom persisted, thank God, so we agreed to keep an eye on the developing news story and ramp up our preparations as necessary.

As COVID-19 started to spread throughout the world and made its way to the U.S., we decided we would have a mandatory remote work day on Monday, March 16th, in which everyone would work from home as a test in the event we would have to shut down for a few days or possibly a week. On Friday the 13th, we had an all-hands meeting where we explained what we knew so far about COVID-19, what our plan was for this day to test working from home, and what I thought would happen going forward—boy, was I wrong. However, as I learned later, the fact that I was wrong didn't matter much to my team. What mattered was that I was willing to share everything I knew, was honest about what I didn't know, and shared the plan that we had so far with some vulnerability—we didn't have all the answers but would do our best to get answers.

As we all know, the weekend of March 14th and 15th saw a significant increase in COVID-19 cases in the NYC area as well as in many other parts of the country. So, our test day turned out to be a mandate from the city of New York as the mayor announced that all non-essential businesses stay home on Monday, March 16th.

As the temporary shutdown of all non-essential business extended beyond the first week and then beyond the first month, that all-hands meeting we had on Friday, March 13th, turned into a weekly all-hands virtual meeting where we continued to share what we knew, what we planned on doing moving forward, and more importantly, why.

One of the greatest common responses we received from our team members during the pandemic was that they felt safe and secure in their jobs because we were very transparent. We certainly weren't always right. We even joked about how many times I predicted that we would be back in the office the following week, only for the mayor of NYC to hold a press conference at the same time extending the shutdown. Whether I was right or wrong mattered less than the fact that we were all in this together and fully transparent. After all, as Patrick Lencioni says, "Vulnerability is a core ingredient to trust."

Another example of the transparency that helped the team feel safe and secure was the fact that, courtesy of our EOS Scorecard, we shared our cash balance with the team. So when COVID hit, the team knew that we had enough cash to cover payroll for four and a half months, plus a line of credit that would extend well beyond that. When our team members heard of friends in and out of our industry being laid off in late March and early April, they were confident in their employment based on our initial and continued discussion.

We told the team that Mary Jo and I had no intention of taking money out of the business, and we would keep everyone employed as long as we all worked with the same individual mindset: "not just to keep ourselves employed but to keep everyone else on the team employed also."

To be fair, our industry is compliance-driven, meaning the work we perform is largely driven by inspections that are required. So, we had some degree of confidence that our work would not stop altogether, and with our industry's recession-resilient history, we felt confident revenue would come back fairly quickly. Our leadership team immediately delegated all items on our annual winter-to-do list that weren't completed the previous winter and accelerated many of the annual goals that we had set for 2020. We shared with the team that we wanted to get as many of these items done while our billable work was limited so that when we are back to some semblance of normalcy, we would want to be as billable as possible to make up for the lost revenue and profit during the shutdown.

Our team responded beautifully; they really crushed it. So much so that we had to talk with a few of them and let them know that we appreciated all the hours they were putting in, but they should also take advantage of the shutdown to spend some time with loved ones, etc. There was no need for them to be putting in 60+ hours per week during this time.

Although we had a team of rockstars driven by our core values and common purpose, we had a few new team members who clearly were not. Within the first two weeks of the shutdown, it was clear that they were not committed to getting their work done at home, not focused on keeping everyone else on the team employed, and really not even focused on keeping themselves employed. So we had to part ways with them. Letting team members go has always been and will always be an emotionally challenging decision, but in this particular case, the rest of the team was galvanized and emboldened by the fact that they knew that everyone was doing their best for the entire team. If they weren't making the effort, they would be immediately held accountable. The stakes were too high for anything less.

In addition to the weekly all-hands meetings, our leadership team had a daily call to share updates. We were gathering as much objective and subjective data as we could.

Objective Data: Was our close ratio, the percentage of projects we won versus lost, increasing or decreasing? Was the turnaround time for clients to make decisions on projects increasing or decreasing? We also divided this data up into client types: What was the close ratio for our three different client types: residential, commercial, and institutional? As a result, we were quickly able to see that institutional clients were making decisions much faster, and we had a higher close ratio with them as well, so we focused more of our BD efforts toward institutional clients.

We certainly didn't give up on residential clients because our data showed that they were making decisions just slower than previously. Commercial clients slowed down quite a bit. They are a great sector to work with, so we, of course, didn't give up on them, but our BD efforts for commercial clients were more focused on long-term items like email drip campaigns as opposed to the weekly phone calls to our institutional clients.

Subjective Data: We had our team members speaking weekly to our clients, the contractors, manufacturers we worked with, and other friends in the industry about what they were observing. Had the clients changed their budgets and/or timelines for projects? Fewer projects than we expected were postponed. A few of our clients even decided to accelerate projects while their buildings were empty—that was a very pleasant surprise. Did the contractors have enough manpower available to perform projects when they were expected to start? Would they be able to get the materials needed in time? Did we need to consider substituting materials? Manpower was a big issue initially, and as we all remember, supply chain issues resulted in some significant delays in material. Speaking directly to manufacturer representatives helped us understand which materials would be delayed due to supply chain disruptions, which materials would see a price increase, and which materials would be more readily available for us to consider or suggest for substitution. As for friends in the industry, we were able to talk with them about many non-confidential, non-proprietary issues to learn how they were solving them, what they anticipated would happen with their project timelines, etc.

Of course, these discussions were open dialogues where we shared what we were observing too. JFK's famous quote, "A rising tide raises all ships," was a common theme we always felt was critical especially during those difficult days.

These conversations were key to our team not just surviving but thriving and growing during the pandemic. We learned early on that many of our competitors laid off some really great people with a wealth of experience. We also felt confident that our clients and the contractors we worked with would be eager to get projects started ASAP, so we hired some rock stars that we might not have otherwise been able to recruit.

As weeks turned into months, our leadership team consistently reiterated our objective of using data and facts to make decisions, not fear and emotion. We certainly wouldn't pretend that we were immune to the normal human emotions playing out during those days, but because we started every daily meeting and weekly all-hands meetings stating that objective, we were quickly able to identify and separate fear and emotion from facts and data. We tried to think through as many possible realistic scenarios and decide what to do in advance so that as issues came up, we could then just execute with no real decisions to make while emotions were high.

A great tool we used to help with that was one developed by Dan Sullivan of Strategic Coach called the First 100 Days plan. As the name implies, we developed a comprehensive plan of what we would do within the first one hundred days of the COVID-19 shutdown being lifted, who would be responsible for each item, and when they would have to complete it (by the 20th day, 50th day, etc.). This plan was essential for the success and growth we experienced. Of course, we didn't execute 100 percent of the plan; some items just didn't happen, and some turned out not to be necessary, but we accomplished the most important aspects of the plan for sure.

As we made our way into July and August of 2020, I observed that it appeared several team members lost appreciation for the fact that we kept the entire team employed during the first few difficult months of COVID-19. This was exacerbated by two team members leaving for higher-paying opportunities at firms that laid off a significant number of employees within weeks of the COVID shutdown. On the other end, admittedly, I started to lose my appreciation for our team members' dedication during that same period, whether they were putting in extra hours or visiting job sites with many COVID-19 restrictions. So, during our weekly all-hands meeting, I shared these observations, and collectively, we decided to add "Appreciation" to our theme for the year, which we highlighted in our all-hands meetings. Each week, we simply reminded ourselves to appreciate each other and what each of us was going through and extended that reminder to our families and loved ones. This constant reminder helped resolve that issue for me and many on the team.

At the start of the COVID-19 pandemic, our philosophy of having no debt, enough cash in the business for an emergency fund, as well as a line of credit to back it up, paid dividends. We were able to make decisions based on what we saw in front of us—what the reality was—and we were able to do it calmly and keep everyone employed because we didn't have the weight of any crushing debt. I know many business owners that, due to the fear of the pandemic, the unknown of the future, combined with the weight of debt, caused them to make the heartbreaking decision of laying off team members and negatively impacting their potential for future growth because of their debt.

How prepared are you for the inevitable emergency? What should you do to help your business survive? What should you do to protect your family?

Dear Brian,

In February 2021, only ten months after bringing our Gracie girl home from Haiti, Finn was scheduled for his tenth surgery due to the Spina Bifida he was born with. This procedure, although very involved and extremely painful, would be a total game changer for our little Finn's quality of life. Signing on to see him go through the pain and recovery is never an easy step, but you, our family visionary, always remind me of the long-term positives of having to go through things like this. It is at times like this I love how our differences can be so complimentary of one another. I have the medical knowledge but the heart of a mom, and you are the strength, always looking at all the good that will come down the road from our present sacrifices or crosses.

We initially met Dr. Alam, Finn's urologist, in Manhattan. I thank God every day he sent Dr. Alam to us. He is an absolute angel walking this Earth. Dr. Alam's vocation as a pediatric urologist has not only saved but given immeasurable quality to so many children's lives around the world, just like Finn. It was a no-brainer to you and me that when Dr. Alam relocated his practice to Charleston, South Carolina, Finn would remain his patient.

A few days prior to Finn's surgery date, the three of us drove down to Charleston to meet with Dr. Alam to review the exact procedure and sign consents. Finn was going to be in Charleston for three weeks following the surgery. You and I talked at length and came up with a game plan that made the most sense for our family. You would stay with Finn during his time in Charleston, and I would fly home to NJ after our meeting with Dr. Alam and take care of the rest of the crew at home. Again, I couldn't be more grateful at times like this. You owned the business and had worked so hard to get the company to this point—the point where you could leave NJ and know you had the right people in place to handle the business's day-to-day up in New York, while you could manage everything you needed from Finn's bedside with your laptop.

Dr. Alam walked into the room with a smile that always made us smile from ear to ear. He reviewed all the intricacies of the surgery, what Finn's two-day pre-op prep would entail, any foreseeable surgical complications, and what Finn's two-week recovery in the hospital would look like. Now, mind you, this was the same conversation we had with Dr. Alam virtually back in January from our home in NJ. After Dr. Alam finished speaking, and you and I signed the consent, he asked who was staying for the three weeks with Finn. I looked at you and said, "I am." You burst out in a little chuckle, and Dr. Alam looked puzzled. You didn't need me to say a word, Brian. You knew after talking to Dr. Alam, hearing exactly what he told us virtually the month prior, that I couldn't leave Finn. So, instead of working at Finn's bedside while you assisted him through the surgery and recovery, you were flying home that night to operate our family's day-to-day for the next three weeks.

I could throw myself under the bus and say, after almost eighteen years of marriage at the time, you had grown accustomed to my flightiness and changing plans on the dime. Or I could say you fully embraced all that it is to be in a sound, faith-filled marriage. Probably a little bit of both! I told Dr. Alam my mom always says, "We make plans and God laughs." Brian, I love how you and I can sit and communicate and draw up plans for any situation that arises, but what I love more is our ability to pivot at the last second and accommodate what is best for our family, even though it is far from our original, well-thought-out, methodical plan. You and I make our plans, and then we leave plenty of room for our Lord to come in and make things right.

Finn's surgery was a complete miracle of a success. I pray for Dr. Alam every day of my life; he is a gift to our world. Brian, you returned to Charleston two weeks later with the same smile you left Finn and me. You ran the house, ran the business, and then decided you would bring Dolan and Grace back to Charleston with you. You told me they needed to see me, and I needed to see them, and you knew how much it would cheer Finn up to see them.

Brian, you embrace our marriage and every curveball I've thrown at you for the past twenty years.

I love you with all my heart,
MJ

Looking at the Future

As we continued growing, we started to contemplate acquiring other firms as a way to tackle our increasing hiring needs and our expansion into different geographic markets. Given the right situation, we thought that might be the best path. We also knew that many of our competitors were firms started by Baby Boomers approaching retirement age, who may not have had a transition plan in place. So, we thought this could be a way to benefit both teams. We could onboard quite a few new team members with existing clients and existing revenue while providing those owners a path to retirement.

So, we started meeting with various target companies and people who might know firms that were interested in selling and had some pretty good results. But we also knew that we didn't know the first thing about the acquisition process. So, we spoke to some advisors and also decided to start meeting with some of the firms that expressed interest in acquiring us.

From the moment we made it to the Inc. 5000 list and Zweig's Hot Firm list, we started getting calls from search firms, private equity firms, and competitors interested in purchasing us. I was always open to those calls so I could learn, hear the types of questions they were asking, find out who else in our industry was looking to acquire, and just be a sponge.

Some of these calls, to be honest, were a little bit of a waste of time; they were people just starting their search process or trying to gather information about our niche. Others were trying to gain competitive insight. But for the most part, the calls were pretty valuable, and they were worth my time. I started to understand the patterns, the types of questions they were asking, and what type of information they were looking for, which then was the type of information I should be looking for as well. All in all, it was definitely worth the exercise, especially when, in 2020, I received an email from Kamal, a gentleman at a larger engineering firm backed by Private Equity that was looking to make a strategic acquisition.

This email had a very different tone to it. Kamal was friendly but had the tone of an obviously serious buyer who was not interested in wasting anyone's time but was very interested in acquiring our firm. I decided to meet with him for lunch, initially, just to better understand the acquisition process. But as lunch started to get closer, my wheels started turning, and the apparent similarities between myself and Kamal, and my firm and his, started to become more clear. Additionally, it was starting to be more clear that the COVID shutdowns were going to have a longer duration than anticipated; this was becoming a marathon, not a sprint as we initially thought. So, considering options to help the business survive and maybe get some reward for the family seemed like a prudent move.

In June 2020, we had lunch. It was a great conversation, and it moved forward to the next steps, where I provided some basic information on our firm, some of it financial and some of it related to our projected growth. They issued a letter of intent to purchase our firm. Receiving the LOI was a very surreal experience, which led to lots of thought and discussions with Mary Jo. Ultimately, we decided to turn it down. While it was a good offer, it just didn't feel right to us. Although we were still in the thick of the COVID pandemic, things were going relatively well.

As we went through the winter of 2020 into 2021, I continued to think about the offer. I thought about some of the struggles we were having as a team, as well as some of the struggles that individuals on our team were having. And I started to contrast what those situations would be like if we stood on the shoulders of a larger organization. In February 2021, I remember waking in the middle of the night to this strong feeling that God was telling me that if we sold the business, we would all be very happy in two to three years. A few weeks later, I woke up in the middle of the night again with that same feeling that God was calling me, this time with more clarity—not just my family, but my entire team would be very happy three years from now.

I'd like to say that I acted on that immediately, but I didn't. I continued to think about it and pray about it. And then, lo and behold, in April 2021, Kamal reached out again. Our industry was compliance-driven, meaning that the work we were involved in was legally mandated to be performed. As a result, and because of the strategic planning we did during COVID, we were very fortunate to have some significant growth between 2020 and 2021. Kamal had been watching our activity and recognized that growth. So when they came back, they were more excited about the opportunity, and internally, so was I.

Mary Jo and I thought and prayed about the decision for weeks and talked about it . . . a lot. We discussed the pros and cons of various different aspects. We recognized that I would likely be much more present with her and the kids after a sale, we would be able to focus our attention on other ventures that we had been contemplating, and, of course, we would remove a good bit of financial risk off the table. We knew that to do this we were trading in the prospect for significant future financial gain had we just stayed and continued to grow the business. We also knew that this was a departure from the initial plan, so it would have a big emotional hit on the team and me, but the prospect for potential new avenues of growth for our team standing on the shoulders of a larger organization appeared to outweigh the emotional hit. We went back and forth, looked at the decision from many different angles, and spoke to many trusted friends and associates who had been in similar positions. Together, we made the fateful decision to sell.

So, at the end of July 2021, our firm was acquired, and we started this new path of determining what Mary Jo and I would do next.

What would you do if an interested buyer approached you about your business? Would you entertain their offer? Why?

The Sale

On July 31, 2021, the closing for the sale of the business occurred. COVID was still making travel complicated, so the closing was handled virtually. It was as anti-climactic as you could imagine. I've heard that all of these closings are very anticlimactic, whether they're in person or done virtually. All of the paperwork is done in advance, and all contracts have been thoroughly reviewed and signed by all parties the day before. The wire transfers are ready, the attorneys have confirmed that all is approved, and everyone on the call has to acknowledge their approval and their receipt of all documents. Then, the wire transfer is sent.

All in all, the call was seven minutes long. It was a very nervous moment but a very exciting moment at the same time. I remember Mary Jo and the kids were home waiting downstairs. When I walked downstairs so soon after the call started, Mary Jo asked what happened. She thought maybe it was canceled or delayed. I said, "No, it's over. That's it." I hugged the kids and Mary Jo, and we went outside and took a selfie. That was it.

Later that night, Mary Jo and I decided to go out to dinner to celebrate. As we got in the car to drive, I could literally feel my shoulders loosen up. Mary Jo commented on it. She said that I looked so much more relaxed. I did. As a husband and father, the tension of worrying about the kids' future, financially at least, went away. It was a surreal feeling and an incredible feeling. As a business owner, the rewards are fantastic, but the stress of wondering whether or not the shoe could drop, whether or not it could all go away at any given moment, is very real. At least for the time being, that feeling was gone. Of course, I traded away future earnings for the immediate reward of the sale, but in my heart, I felt then, and I still feel now, that it was the best move for me and my family. We enjoyed a great dinner and relaxed conversation as we celebrated that night at our favorite local steakhouse, the same one where we had our early anniversary dinners.

Mary Jo and I talked about not making any hasty decisions and seeing how the next few years would go. Perhaps I'd want to stay with the acquiring firm long term; perhaps I'd want to figure out an opportunity where I could work part-time with them and chase new endeavors. Or perhaps I would want to just leave after two years and solely focus on new endeavors.

We knew that one of our goals was to help other couples start their small businesses. So, we have started down that path, trying to remember to take it slow and see where God is calling us.

At the advice of several people, I had been paying attention to my thoughts on the sale of the business, and it was interesting to note how the emotions ranged from initial happiness and contentment to moments of seller's remorse, with occasional feelings that I was no longer bringing the family the value I previously did as a business owner. The negative thoughts were not very frequent and quickly subsided. For the most part, the feelings were contentment in the present moment, something I struggled with while running the business, and an optimistic curiosity about the future, something I've always enjoyed.

Dear Brian,

The summer of 2021 was such an amazing gift of a summer. We moved out of our home in June, the last day of school for the kids and the official start of summer vacation. The dream we had talked about since we had married, of someday building our family home, was coming to fruition. You were in the final stages of selling the business. You spent countless hours on the phone in final negotiation conversations and transition meetings; the folding table you were using as a desk was in the master bedroom of our temporary townhouse rental. There was so much excitement with the summer finally here, the house demo/reno well underway, and the sale of the business.

The week after you sold the company, we spent three weeks in the Outer Banks of North Carolina to get the kids out of the townhouse for a little bit. We packed up our two cars to the max, and with the six kids and the two dogs, we pulled out of the townhouse complex when it was still dark in the morning. We were all so excited. As I was driving, I was sort of kicking myself for not getting the kids' school uniforms before we left. I knew there wouldn't be enough time to get them fitted when we got back from NC and get them in time for the first day of school. I don't pat myself on the back for much, but I know you totally agree with me when I say I've perfected the art of procrastination. So, I couldn't understand why I was getting this unrelenting nagging feeling about the uniforms. The car was quiet, and I was praying to try to get my mind on something else, but my mind just kept floating back to the kids and their school.

The kids' school and the parish had become our second home and our second family. Over the past fifteen years, I believed sometimes the hours we spent there were more than we were at home. I was always so grateful to God that it was a stone's throw away from our house since we were there all the time. But the time had come for our family to move on; I knew that, and you did as well. I had been praying all summer long for God to guide my heart. I knew what that nagging feeling in the car ride to the Outer Banks was: it was God telling us it was time to move on. But where were we going to send the kids now? Our expectations for a Catholic school were high; we wanted it all from their school. We wanted a sound academic education but, more so, one rooted in Catholic tradition. We wanted our faith and our Lord intertwined in every aspect of their school day.

Upon our arrival at the house in NC, I carved out a little time each day to pray and research other Catholic elementary school options for our four youngest. I remember calling my brother, Fr. Ed, to bounce my thoughts off of him. He was so patient, letting me speak and offering his input; I valued his opinion as a Catholic priest so much, and he knew how heavy this decision was weighing on me. You, Brian, are my confidant, my go to, but you were still buzzing from the sale that just went through literally days prior to our arrival in NC. Although you were just as frustrated with the parish and the school as I was, I wanted you to have a clear mind prior to me discussing it with you. I also knew it was important we take time to celebrate the amazing accomplishment of the sale of the company before we attempt to solve this challenge. Before I presented my concerns to you, I wanted to find some potential answers and options for us to even consider this change.

I knew this was a "bring me a solution, not a problem" instance, a phrase I had heard you refer to many times on your entrepreneurial journey. From my research, one school stood out from the rest, so I immediately called them. When I hung up the phone, I said out loud, "Thank you, Lord." I set up a Zoom call with the headmaster for the morning after, and all that was left to do was speak to you.

While walking on the beach, I explained my concerns and this uneasy feeling I was having about the children returning to their current school. You listened patiently and agreed to sit in on the Zoom meeting with me. During the meeting, we both looked at each other with this expression of relief. God had led us to our family's next chapter, Our Lady of Mount Carmel in Boonton, NJ, a beautiful new elementary school as well as a flourishing parish enriched in the deep Catholic tradition—AMEN! We enrolled them as soon as the meeting concluded.

We mutually decided to let the kids enjoy their last few days at the beach, and we would tell them on the drive home. The only reason for the urgency to tell them on the ride home was because their first day at their new school would be the next morning. They took the news like champs. Dolan was super quiet—he's our internal thinker. Finn was rapid-fire with questions. Julia was somewhere in the middle of the two boys, just trying to grasp the fact that when she woke up the next morning, she'd be starting a new middle school. And Grace, as in all things, was super excited. I'll never forget the three older children's faces when they lined up that morning with their new classes. They had all of 24 hours to absorb this huge change in their lives.

You and I stood there, trying to keep it together; if there was ever a doubting moment in our parenting, this was it! They were so incredibly brave and supportive of you and me for changing their school. My heart broke for them on one hand, but on the other, I couldn't have been more proud of them and how they responded to our decision. Each day got a little easier, and even though we knew this was a challenge for them, they never questioned our decision. They had complete trust in you and me that, together, we would only make the best decisions for them. I think they also know that all of our decisions go through our Lord, and they rest assured in that. God is so good. We found this exceptional, growing, and flourishing Catholic school and parish that has been such a gift to our family. I'm so grateful we had the courage to leave something that was changing but had been so comfortable for 15 years in search of something more. Sitting in Mass this past Sunday, listening to another one of Fr. Daniel's beautiful and challenging sermons, with 11 altar servers, two of our boys included, and seeing all the beautiful friends we have met, God reassured me that collectively, with his Love and guidance, we made the right decision for our family.

I love you,
MJ

Who is your Fr. Daniel?
Is your current faith community in line with your values?
Is it challenging you to be the best version of yourself?
Or is it simply good enough?

Radical Generosity

Just like all other forms of personal and professional growth, when we step out of our comfort zone, we are stretched to new capabilities, grow, and adopt a new normal. Recently, I was asked to give a "call to heart" talk prior to a fundraising event at our church. The event was attended by a great group of devout Catholics I love and respect deeply. So, when I was first asked, my gut reaction was, "I'm sure there's somebody else better. Maybe I'll be ready next year." But when I thought more about it, I realized that to accomplish greatness, we have to push ourselves beyond our comfort zone. Our parish community is accomplishing greatness every day, and the Pastor's vision will magnify that greatness for the benefit of many. So I needed to do my small part and give the talk.

There have been several times in the past twenty years when Mary Jo and I have decided to give outside of our comfort zone. We committed to a donation that was a stretch, and we'd look at each other, wondering whether or not we could afford it. But every single time, that level of giving became our new normal. The feeling of giving is fantastic; the feeling of giving outside of our comfort zone has always had a much more lasting impact on us, resulting in us being more committed to the cause we were supporting. The enjoyment of that involvement alone was worth the financial investment, let alone knowing the good that money would do.

Mary Jo and I have witnessed that the more generous we are to serve God, the more blessings he bestows on us. After all, as Dave Ramsey says, "The money in our wallets, purses, and bank accounts isn't ours—it's God's. He's just letting us be a steward, which is the Bible's way of saying God lets us manage (not own) His money."

How would you define your generosity? Do you regularly push yourself outside your comfort zone?

Dear Brian,

While sitting in the pews of Our Lady of Mount Carmel Church, we have heard Fr. Daniel speak of radical generosity more times than I could ever count. I remember the first time hearing him speak the words. I thought about how radical generosity is a theme woven throughout the entire Bible; there is no debating that, but I still recall being struck by the words. I remember Fr. Daniel saying, in a much more profound and eloquent manner, that radical generosity defines us as disciples of Jesus Christ. I looked at you, Brian, sitting in the pew with all the kids and thought, My goodness, you are fully committed to radical generosity.

You brought radical generosity into our home at a very early stage of our marriage, and you've made it a driving force for your business, our family, and the decisions we make. It was in the dawning phase of the business that you approached me about being more generous as a couple and a family. I remember thinking that you were absolutely right but, at the same time, in complete awe. You were barely keeping your head above water, working 100+ hours a week, and this is where your heart was sitting. You got a small glimpse of your company starting to make it, and your heart automatically turned to radical generosity. Through your exhaustion and the stress of operating a new and now quickly growing company while balancing a marriage as well as a family with five kids at the time, your mind was on God and all the gifts he had given us. Your constant connection with our Lord and the solid foundation provided to you by your parents maintained that realization that what we are given is not ours. And being grateful to our Lord for all these gifts made it possible for us to give in a radical way. As Dr. Kenneth Boa references in his book Leverage, it is the "currency of Heaven." Dr. Boa writes, "Radical generosity is an internal investment. As God gives to us, so we are to give to others. We transmute the currency of the temporal into the currency of the eternal by investing in our relationships. People will last, money does not; give for the sake of His Kingdom."[11] This is where your heart was sitting, Brian, and so came the birth of a beautiful relationship with our dear friend Carlos.

After being rejected by multiple organizations that wouldn't allow us to bring the kids to volunteer, I reached out to Carlos Roldan, the director of the food pantry at the Father English Center in Paterson. I asked him if it would be okay if you and I brought the kids down to the food pantry with some groceries. Carlos replied, "Yes, of course." He met us at the door with our packages. The kids were 6, 7, 9, 11, and 13 at the time. Carlos insisted the kids stay to load the shelves. He took so much time telling them how much happiness the food they brought was going to bring a family in need. No matter how crazy your schedule was back then, Brian, mark my words, we were at Stop & Shop every two weeks with the kids loading shopping carts to bring to the Father English Center. Our relationship with Carlos and the Father English Center flourished and grew as our family and the business also grew. Through your heart and your radical generosity, Brian, God brought Carlos into our lives and our children's lives. Our children have become witnesses to overwhelming compassion, kindness, and generosity over the past six years from Carlos and his work at the Father English Center. The people Carlos has brought into our lives have blessed us in more ways imaginable. Carlos is a man of God, doing so much to help our community. I thank God every day that your heart, Brian, led us to him.

I was reluctant to turn down this path in my writing. The Bible teaches us in Matthew 6:1-4, "Be careful not to display your righteousness merely to be seen by people. Otherwise, you have no reward in heaven. Thus whenever you do charitable giving, do not blow a trumpet before you. But when you do your giving, do not let your left hand know what your right hand is doing so that your gift may be in secret." But there is a deep part of me that believes that if everyone starting a business shares your radical generosity and discipleship to Jesus, Brian, then success is imminent. Your humility that comes with your generosity is profound. You give of yourself, your resources, and your time constantly. But you are a light that other business owners should want to emulate, in my biased mind.

Our dear friend Carlos put it so beautifully a few months ago. You shared with Carlos how you sold your business as well as sharing all the exciting future business endeavors you have planned. Carlos simply replied, "I hope all your future endeavors bring you great financial success because I know how much good in the world will come from you." That is a legacy worth mentioning. I am so proud to be your wife.

I love you,
MJ

Who is your Carlos?
What organizations are near you that your time, your money, and your heart will provide a great reward for others and an even bigger reward for you?

Hey Mary Jo,

Our strong faith in God and each other has been established throughout our lives, and our marriage seems to become more and more critical with every passing year. The faith we had in God to protect us and the business during the COVID pandemic was critical. As was His guidance when we were making the very large decision to change our parish community; after all, we have both only been members of two parishes our entire lives.

Now, of course, we didn't leave it all in God's hands. We put in the effort to do the due diligence and the hard work; we left no stone unturned, but we did so with the love and support of God the Father.

We recently heard the fable from Fr. Juan at a Regnum Christi gala of two monks who were standing in a decrepit garden. As I recall the story, the first monk asked the other, "Whose garden is this?" "God owns this garden," the second monk replied. Then, the first monk asked, "Who's responsible for this garden?" The second monk said, "God is responsible for this garden." Well, the first monk was not pleased with this, so he took responsibility for the garden. Over the years, the once decrepit garden began to flourish. Years later, a third monk came along and asked the first, "Whose garden is this?" The first monk replied, "God owns this garden." Then the third monk asked, "Who's responsible for this garden?" The first monk proudly responded, "I am responsible for this garden." The third monk complimented the garden, and the first replied even more proudly, "Well, you should've seen the sorry state it was in when God was responsible."

We all had a good laugh, but the message was delivered: God owns the garden, but we are the gardeners. This little story is a great indication of how we are trying to live our lives, raise our family, and run the business.

Love,
Brian

VI

ADULTHOOD

We know that all things work together for good for those who love God, who are called according to his purpose.

—Romans 8:28

You have a limited number of heartbeats in your life; it is a finite number. And you have a limited number of steps you're going to take in your life; it's a finite number and it can be calculated. The question is, what is your heart beating for, and where are your steps taking you?

—Fr. Rich Frechette

Dear Brian,

You and I equally adore this quote. It was written by an exceptional man and mark my word, someday will be a saint, Fr. Rick Frechette. His story is remarkable, and the work he has done in Haiti and the countless lives he has saved is astonishing!

This quote just says it all. God put you and me on this Earth and gave us a purpose. Our faith fostered by our parents allows our hearts to be open to this purpose. Our marriage is built on that purpose. It's our responsibility as a couple to hold each other

> *accountable to that purpose; a constant reminder to one another what our hearts are beating for and where our steps are taking us!*
>
> *I love you,*
> *MJ*

As we transition into this next phase, post-starting, growing, and selling our first business, to what lies ahead, the word that keeps coming up over and over for us is intentionality. We recognize that this opportunity to reset and refocus our priorities is a gift from God that we do not want to waste. So, we want to be very intentional about who we spend our time, talent, and treasure with and how we spend it. The theme running through our lives right now is: Slow down to speed up and see where God is calling us.

Like many entrepreneurs, I have the natural tendency to want to jump from one venture to the next. I started work full time the Monday after graduating from college. Whenever I left one job for another, my last day would be on a Friday, and I'd start at the new place on the next Monday. I'm realizing that with all that running, perhaps I wasn't always hearing where God was calling me to go.

The natural inclination to jump, coupled with the feelings of lack of purpose that have crept in while not having a day-to-day job, could definitely cause me to make a poor decision. Fortunately, several trusted friends brought this concern to my attention very early on in the process of selling our business, so I decided to start working with a performance coach.

I was introduced to Vince Fowler and immediately realized the benefit his wealth of coaching experience, individual drive, and calming demeanor would have for me. Our weekly virtual calls tend to help me stay accountable for priority tasks, stay grounded, and avoid chasing new opportunities that don't make sense for our future goals.

The more I've invested in education and coaching, the more I've grown and accomplished. My parents started the investment in my education for elementary school, high school, and college, and I continued that mindset with traditional programs in graduate school and the Harvard Business school program. Additionally, I pursued further education in less traditional avenues, such as professional coaching with the local forum group, then continued it with the Executives Association, EOS, Strategic Coach, and now Vince. This may seem excessive to some—it likely would've seemed that way to me fifteen years ago as well. I try to remember that the bigger my vision, the more help and wisdom from others I need to get there. As Jim Rohn stated, "Learning is the beginning of wealth. Learning is the beginning of health. Learning is the beginning of spirituality. Searching and learning is where the miracle process all begins."

One of the concepts Vince and I have been discussing quite a bit is the concept of a gap year/sabbatical for professionals, especially entrepreneurs. This time away would be an amplified version of the Free Days concept in Strategic Coach, where the preparation for the time away and then the execution of it would likely result in a business permanently running more independently from the entrepreneur.

Something very relevant for me right now is the idea of adjusting my career from being a doer to more of a mentor or adviser. This idea is discussed in more detail and more eloquently in Arthur Brooks's book *From Strength to Strength*. Arthur describes how our fluid intelligence curve, which allows us to analyze things or break them apart, starts to decline in our mid-forties to our mid-fifties. This intersects with our simultaneously rising crystallized intelligence curve, which allows us to synthesize or put things together.[12] Our fluid intelligence is what we typically think of as intelligence in school and work, while crystallized intelligence is our wisdom gained from years of experience.

Using a sabbatical or gap year to transition from the first part of our entrepreneurial journey to the next seems like a logical transition that allows for the proper time away, refocusing on priorities, and listening to where God calls us; at least, I sure hope it is.

What is your heart beating for, and where are your steps taking you?
Do you need some time to think it through? Are you being intentional with your time, talent, and treasure? Are you intentional with those you spend your time with?

Small Business Incubator

Mary Jo and I decided to start a small business incubator focused on helping existing and aspiring entrepreneurial couples grow their business while building strong families and nurturing abundant faith. We are using our experiences, resources, and network to help as many couples as possible fulfill their Vision and then expand it further while avoiding some of the mistakes that we made and helping them navigate their own mistakes.

Recalling how difficult the early days were when we were starting our company, despite the fact that we had a strong support system to lean on, we recognized additional resources would've been very beneficial to us back then. As such, our small business incubator aspires to bring mentorship, coaching, office and collaboration space, and an enhanced professional network to support the business aspects of the journey. Additionally, we provide support and guidance to help strengthen the family and faith aspects of the Entrepreneurial Trinity as well.

Who is your ideal support system?
Do you have your rock? Do you have mentors? How strong is your network? Should you reach out to a small business incubator in your area?

Couples Connection®

Strategic Coach has a workshop called Couples Connection that allows couples to spend some really dedicated time thinking about their bigger future, setting their goals, learning how their strengths and weaknesses should be complementary rather than confrontational, learning other methods of how to communicate better, and how to continue to grow in love through the five freedoms: health, time, money, purpose, and relationship.

It seems strange, but much like business coaching, taking the time away to dedicate ourselves to growing as a couple and being in line was incredibly valuable for the long-term benefit of our family. We knew we had complementary skills, and intuitively, we kind of got it as we went. But until then, we hadn't seen it on paper; we hadn't discussed those complementary strengths and weaknesses. By looking at these more closely in the workshop, we realized that when the stress was high, sometimes those complementary weaknesses led to confrontation. However, when we were working on something important, those complementary strengths were exactly what helped us be stronger as a couple and achieve a better end result. We came away from the workshop with an effective way to communicate about these strengths and weaknesses.

Mary Jo came up with the analogy that we had been driving down the same highway heading in the same direction. However, we were in two separate cars on parallel paths. After attending Couples Connections and creating our plan for moving forward, including weekly meetings and quarterly half-day sessions, we are in the same car, driving together towards that same goal. No doubt, we will get there faster, easier, and with a lot more fun.

One of the things that we think was a success and why we were able to continue to head in the same direction, although we weren't intentional about discussing our strengths and weaknesses, was that we attempted to recognize most of the time that we were both trying to go in that same general direction. We weren't competing with each other, and we didn't assume that there was malintent. When one of us may have appeared like we were veering off at an exit ramp, we were fairly good at understanding each other, putting ourselves in each other's shoes, and correcting to get us back on the same highway.

Dear Brian,

I sat down at the table in the large conference room that first morning in San Diego, California, looked around the room, and asked myself, "What am I doing here?" I felt so out of place. You had asked me years ago about my feelings about attending a Couples Connection weekend seminar. You had attended Strategic Coach for years, and I knew the impact it had on you personally and professionally. I listened to countless stories for years of all the people you met and all the amazing things they were doing, as well as all the sound advice they had given you. Coach was truly impactful for you and the business. I was definitely open to Couples Connection; it seemed like a great opportunity to meet some powerful couples and really get inspired, there was no doubt about that. What I feared most was not only leaving the kids for four straight days but just this nagging feeling of "this really is not my thing." Let's be honest; you're the extrovert, Brian, the networker, the people-person. It is actually fuel for your soul to hear other people's passions and drives and obtain others' feedback on your visions and ideas. This is just not me. I was intimidated and nervous.

We had actually been booked to attend the Couples Connection seminar in Arizona five years prior. A month before going, I asked you to cancel. I let that uneasy feeling about stepping outside my comfort zone get the best of me, and you obliged and canceled the trip. But I could hear you on the phone, and as you canceled, you said, "Just give us a credit. We'll be at the next one." I love your perseverance and the confidence you have in me that I don't even have in myself. So, when the dates came out for the Couples Connection in California, I knew there was no squirming out of this one. It was a different time for us. You had sold the business a year prior, we had finished the house renovation, and were back living in our house; the timing was just perfect, all I needed to do was get the courage to go.

I sat there at the table, overlooking the beautiful Pacific Ocean that morning with this big binder in front of me, you next to me, and four couples I had never met. I nervously flipped through the binder and noticed a large amount of blank spaces for writing/journaling. I felt so vulnerable at that moment, like this was finally going to be the aha moment for you that I married someone way out of my league. The moderator for the seminar started the morning with a prayer, and I thought to myself, Dear Jesus, Please let my heart be filled with gratitude to have such an amazing husband who wants to share this experience with me. Let my heart and mind be open to what's about to unfold here. I'm not going to lie; those first few exercises that morning were extremely difficult. I was struggling, but you picked up on that. You were so patient and encouraging, gently pulling my words out of me.

Two hours into the day, I was sitting on the edge of my seat, looking down at the paper you and I had just written: our 3-year plan, our 5-year plan, and our 10-year plan. It was such an amazing point in our marriage. After those exercises, I told you it felt like we finally got in the same car. The previous 19 years had felt as if we were in separate cars, in parallel lanes, both going the same direction, heading towards the same destiny, just in separate cars, you running the business, me running the bulk of the family. After 19 years, it was there at the table of our first Couple's Connection when it felt like we finally jumped in the same car. We were pumped. I was so grateful to our Lord for giving us this moment and opening my eyes and heart to your love and intentions for our marriage.

Another powerful exercise we did at Couples Connection was the Print® Survey. This self-assessment gave us a breakdown of our individual personality traits: unconscious motivators, shadow behaviors, triggers, strengths, and weaknesses. Really such an impactful study, especially getting to see our two assessments side by side and how completely different/opposite our Print Surveys compliment our marriage. We joked about the house renovation, how when we would speak to Spencer, our amazing house contractor, about details, you would wander off because small details are not your thing; you're big picture, our visionary. Then, you would wander back and check on me. You knew the details were my wheelhouse and could step away. Seeing these traits on paper in front of us that weekend and understanding our two complementary personalities helped us understand how well we work together, how our two different Prints emboldened the success of the business, and also gave us the confidence for future businesses we'll start together.

The Couples Connection left a permanent mark on our marriage. We left that weekend stronger, more in love, more grounded, and rooted in our faith in our Lord and in each other. The vision and emphasis for the past 13 years have been mostly on the business. With God's grace and your brilliance, you fulfilled and surpassed your vision for the business, and now it was time to formally create the vision for our marriage and our family.

Thank you, Brian, for pushing me to step outside my comfort zone and believing and investing in me and our marriage. Instead of just hearing all of your wonderful stories from Strategic Coach, I got to experience it for myself in Couples Connection. We met such beautiful and inspiring couples; I will never forget that weekend. And just when you had me good and bought in, you dropped the, "Hey, I'm thinking of writing a business book. Would you write it with me?" And here we are! Can't wait for our next Couple's Connection, babe.

I love you,
MJ

Are you and your spouse headed in the same direction but in separate cars? Are you being intentional about where you're driving your business? Your family? Your faith?

EOS in the Family

After returning from the Couples Connection weekend, Mary Jo and I began developing a way to use EOS to help us accomplish our goals, communicate more consistently, and make sure we stayed on the same page. We didn't start with all-day meetings as EOS would start for a business; we jumped right into weekly meetings. It would've been really hard to find the time in our schedules for multiple long sessions, so I wanted to get some early success with weekly meetings and then go from there. Once we had a full quarter under our belt, it was much easier to make the time for a quarterly session, knowing the value that would come out of the time spent. In hindsight, we may have had even more success if we started the same way that EOS operates for a business; potentially, but perhaps the lack of buy-in would've knocked us off our tracks before we got going.

We are currently in the midst of our third quarter and just completed two 3-hour sessions where we completed our family vision. The clarity that has come from Mary Jo and I clearly identifying what our family's core values are, what we're passionate about, our lifetime wish list, what our 10-year goals are, what life looks like for our family three years from now, and tying all of that into our goals for this year and this quarter is so powerful. In addition to helping plan what we will focus our time and attention on moving forward, using the vision plan as a filter for what we will *not* dedicate our resources towards is even more important. As a result, we even developed our theme for the year: "Slow down to speed up, see where God is calling us."

We also decided to roll out EOS to our three oldest children, all teenagers. The early results that we've had have been staggering to me. The kids really embraced it and jumped in, setting some ambitious quarterly goals, and I felt they really chose the right metrics for themselves. Just like when we roll out any new initiative to our team members, rolling out EOS to our kids required a decent amount of coaching and guidance, but Mary Jo and I attempted to avoid telling them what their Rocks and metrics should be. We simply asked open-ended questions; of course, some were leading and guiding, but I feel like that may only be necessary for the first few quarters. As they've accomplished their goals each quarter, they have already begun setting bigger goals and understanding which areas are the most important to focus on. Some examples of topics that they've used to set Rocks for themselves include college visits and applications, testing out various methods to reduce stress, and attempting to gain confidence through sports, academics, and social interactions. Some of the Scorecard measurables the kids came up with are quality time with siblings and grandparents, quality time in person with friends, exercise, daily prayers, and practicing hobbies.

At the start of each meeting, we share one individual personal best and one best with every other family member in the meeting—so one with me, one with MJ, one with Gavin, etc. This is by far my favorite part of the meeting. It's so fun to hear them all talk about their favorite interactions with each other. It's typically the simple things, like conversations in the car or playing music together.

When we established scoreboard goals, the kids each shared things they wanted to start doing more of like "playing music, playing golf, time with each other, grandparents," so we added those to the Scorecard as weekly metrics. We then asked what they're doing now that they would have to stop to make room for these new priorities, and they all said those magic words: "Less time with electronics." Each time one of them missed their goal for the week, they admitted that they got sucked into their phone or laptop. So, they agreed to help each other out by playing more music together, going outside together, going swimming together, etc. We then observed that rather than us telling the kids to put their devices down and them getting pissed at us, they were inviting each other to do something together.

We are only a few quarters in, so this could fall apart, but so far, I don't see that happening. At this point, the kids and Mary Jo are just as excited about it as I am. I do have a safety net against that, though; our first family quarterly meeting was held in a suite at Citi Field prior to a Mets baseball game. The intent was to give the kids and ourselves a reward for making it through the quarter so successfully, but truthfully, also to help get everyone hyped up for the meeting. It was also a backstop for me in the event that they started to lose interest in the process. Looking back at how quickly they bought into the process, the suite wasn't necessary, but it was such a memorable first quarterly that I'm sure we'll do it again soon.

A friend recently asked me why the kids bought in so quickly and why they were so willing to set goals and be held accountable. So I asked them, and their responses were very similar to how I would imagine our teams at work feel when included as well. *Rather than being told what to do, they liked choosing their quarterly goals and openly discussing them proactively each week instead of randomly getting grilled about them. They liked being included in more mature conversations. They liked learning about the process, about setting goals, and how to accomplish them. They liked knowing what my and Mary Jo's goals were as well as knowing that we were being held accountable by them; previously, it's just been us holding them accountable.*

I've spoken to several friends who own businesses running on EOS, and most have agreed that it makes sense to bring some of the concepts we use to run our business home to our families. After all, our families are by far the most important investment of our time, talent, and treasure, with the best potential return on that investment. However, many have said the same thing: They worry that if they try to initiate these concepts at home, their spouse and/or kids will laugh and think they're a dork. Fortunately for me, Mary Jo and the kids already knew I was a dork, so that wasn't a hurdle. That being said, it did take a bit of courage to first roll it out because I really wanted it to work knowing the benefits it had for me professionally. I wanted those benefits for them personally and for their future careers.

Dear Brian,

"Start on time, end on time. We'll begin with the segue, start with the brave one, and go to the left, one personal best and one professional best." This beginning dialog of your weekly meetings implemented from EOS has been ingrained in my brain since well before you asked me what I thought of implementing EOS in the family. For years, I had listened to you run your virtual meetings with your co-workers in this manner. I remember when you approached me about starting EOS for your company. I loved conversations like these because you already knew what you were going to or needed to do; you just needed to hear yourself telling me about it. Again, I knew my role here, the sounding board, got it! I remember the remarkable change I saw in you professionally and personally soon after the business started implementing EOS. It was extraordinary, and I was fully on board to start implementing it at home.

Starting the weekly meetings was a great transition for both of us from the Couple's Connection. We initially began the meetings just with each other. You thought it would be a good idea to run me through them for a month before bringing the kids on board. You also figured they'd have more buy-in if we told them we were doing them together. You put a ton of work and effort into getting our scoreboard, Rocks, and tasks all up and going. Our meetings provide us with intentional time together, talking about our short-term and long-term individual goals and goals as a couple. I also love the accountability the meetings bring to myself and my actions and tasks.

Soon after starting our meetings with each other, we started the meetings with the three older kids, Gavin (18), Adanya (16), and Julia (14). I could not believe how receptive they were right out of the gate. Now, truth be told, there was a good bit of chuckling from the three of them at the beginning of the first meeting, watching you geek out over the family's meeting agenda and the scoreboard. But you let them have their jabs and proceeded on like a true champ. I have to say the meetings with them over the past year have been one of our biggest gifts. To hear our three teenagers articulating their goals and desires to make themselves better individuals is beyond rewarding. It's a strip-down, judgment-free zone, and the kids know this. We get in these meetings and the kids are looking for truthful, honest feedback. And what I love most is they are giving the feedback right back to you and me.

We are a unit, and if one of us is struggling, we are all struggling. Whether it's Gavin making Rocks to keep his grades where he wants them or Adanya setting tasks to try multiple de-stressors throughout the week to help alleviate some of the stress her junior year loaded with AP courses is placing on her, we are all in this together. One of my favorite parts of the meetings is when Julia reviews the subtasks you helped her set up in her Rock planner. Julia suffers from self-confidence, as we both do. At this point in the meeting, she shares her sub-tasks and asks each one of us for an assessment of herself and how we think she's doing in terms of her self-confidence and managing it. She absorbs this feedback with incredible poise and maturity. I look at her each time we do this exercise with absolute awe. Would I even be brave or mature enough to do this with my family right now at the age of 50? Probably not. These meetings are so powerful and motivating; we all feed off of each other's energy, and we want to do better and be better because we feel we owe it to one another.

You are a gift, Brian. You brought this into our family and have invested a ton of your time and energy into getting it started and keeping it going. I know these meetings are something our children will never forget, and I cannot wait until the others get a little older and start joining. Beyond grateful to our Lord for bringing EOS your way and giving you the insight to fully embrace it when you did.

I love you,
MJ

VII
UNSOLICITED ADVICE

Where there is no guidance, a nation falls, but in an abundance of counselors, there is safety.

—Proverbs 11:14

As mentioned at the start of the book, the intent of this book was to simply share our journey as we started, grew, and ultimately sold our engineering firm while simultaneously growing our family and our faith. However, as we wrote it, we couldn't help but think of advice we would give our younger 35-year-old selves.

I'll apologize in advance because this chapter is a bit random. After all, it is unsolicited advice that often comes at you randomly. So take from it what you feel is valuable and ignore what isn't, just like we should with all unsolicited advice.

Recognizing the Sacrifices

Mary Jo was our rock. She was the glue for the family and kept all the plates spinning seamlessly at home while being my business confidant and cheerleader. She's truly amazing, but I didn't tell her that enough. Throughout each day, week, and month, I was often so focused on my work issues and my busy schedule that I didn't spend enough time assisting or even recognizing all that she was doing and all that she was sacrificing.

When she stopped working as a nurse at Memorial Sloan Kettering, a career she loved and was incredibly gifted at, I was very grateful that she did so. However, to be honest, it took me more time than it should've to recognize that she was not only giving up one of her callings in life, but she was also giving up some of her identity. Furthermore, as a pediatric nurse, the world was losing a phenomenal caregiver to kids battling cancer.

Just typing those words makes me feel like such a clown for not expressing my appreciation more in the moment and not recognizing all of her sacrifices more. Now, she would say she didn't need them or that I recognized them plenty, but I know I should've done more. Back then, I felt guilty that she was leaving the medical industry and her little patients were losing her gifts so that I could grow my engineering firm. It seems like an unfair trade.

I knew that she was doing it to be there for me and the kids, and she stated many times that's what she wanted, but I still felt guilty. In hindsight, it's likely because I wasn't verbally recognizing her many sacrifices enough.

Are you doing enough verbally and non-verbally to show your gratitude to those sacrificing for you and your business?

Mental Well Being

Last year, when I hurt my knee playing basketball, the stress I put on my legs was too much for my 48-year-old knee to take. Fortunately, it wasn't a major injury, but I was limping significantly, and Mary Jo could see the pain that I was in. So, I went to the doctor and then went to weekly physical therapy for three months. One year later, I am still working to strengthen my legs to avoid my knee giving out altogether.

As the stress of business and life accumulated over the years, I typically internalized it. Sometimes, Mary Jo could see it in my behavior and demeanor; sometimes, she could not. Unfortunately, the visual signs of the impact of mental stress aren't as blatant as a physical ailment or injury. We need to be aware of the subtle signs of mental stress and look for them in ourselves, our loved ones, and our team members.

With our team members, sometimes we could tell if they were struggling with mental stress, and sometimes we couldn't. We tried to have open discussions and encourage our team to share with us when they were struggling. We've had many conversations with our team, either virtually, if necessary, but preferably over coffee or lunch. Sometimes, this meant a career change for them; sometimes, it led to them seeking professional help, and other times, the casual conversations with recurring check-ins were enough.

It's common for us as business owners to defer prioritizing our physical health while we focus on the business. Unfortunately, it's even more common that we defer prioritizing our mental health. I've had many conversations with business owners about waking up at night with chest pains, sweating, or not sleeping at all. If we're in pain, we need to make the necessary adjustments to reduce the strain on ourselves and get the expert advice that we need, whether that's from a physical therapist or mental therapist. We should also avoid hiding that pain from our spouse; they likely know something is going on anyway, and they can often be a better judge of when help is needed.

Who are you comfortable speaking about your mental well-being with? Are you equally committed to getting the help you need, whether it is for your knee or your mind?

Spiritual Well Being

Similar to our physical and mental health, we should be aware of and proactive about our spiritual well-being. Like so many of us, I have been very streaky about intentionally spending time with the Lord. During the highs and lows of business and life, I would remember to pray and ask God for guidance and help or thank Him for recent blessings, but when life was relatively status quo, I wasn't as intentional.

To be honest, I suppose I took God for granted. I've recently become more dedicated to a more consistent focus on strengthening my Spiritual health. As Bishop Robert Barron stated in his daily reflection recently. "Jesus declared that he is the vine and we are the branches . . . . The spirit is a living thing, and it derives its life from the vine. If, therefore, you are separated from the vine, you will die spiritually, and you will stop living a supernatural life. And it's just not that complicated."

Fortunately, I have developed a great relationship with our new Pastor and several other priests and religious leaders who are helping me strengthen my faith. Similarly, we have developed strong relationships with other couples whose dedication to their faith inspires and motivates Mary Jo and me. Recently, to continue our growth, we have both begun working with spiritual directors.

Mary Jo started working with her director several months before I did, and through her gentle persuasion and my own witness to her immediate results, I have started working with a director as well. I wasn't certain going in as to the benefit the process would be, but I definitely wanted to improve. A decent analogy, in my mind, is a physical trainer in a gym. We don't need them to show us how to do curls, but they are incredibly helpful at showing us other ways to work on our biceps, how to work on all the muscles in the body and hold us accountable to accomplish our goals. Similarly, my spiritual director is sharing different ways to pray and virtues to focus on, and he's holding me accountable to developing a stronger relationship with God.

Where do you obtain your spiritual direction?
Are the religious leaders in your life pushing you enough and demanding the best of you? Do your friends inspire and motivate you? Would dedicated spiritual direction make sense for you?

Faith at Work

I recently had an in-depth conversation with several faith-filled business owners and leaders about expressing our faith at work. As expected, the feelings on the topic varied significantly. One of the men who is a leader in a very large corporation said that he is not allowed to discuss or display his faith at all. While the owner of a professional services firm shared that he hosts a voluntary daily rosary session in his office conference room. Remarkably, that started when a young woman on his team, who did not regularly pray but was in need of some prayers, asked him to keep her in mind as she knew he was an avid prayer. Rather than simply stating yes, as I would've, he invited the young woman to pray with him. As a result, a beautiful new ritual was formed in their office, and several other team members joined them when they felt so inclined.

Most of us in the discussion fell into a somewhat middle ground, though. One of the men in the discussion summed it up as subscribing to the words of St. Francis: "Preach the Gospel at all times, use words as necessary." I've never been shy about my faith, but I also never tried to force my opinions about faith on anyone, especially captive employees.

When talking about weekend plans, I often described going to mass or another faith-focused event. I had a statue of St. Patrick prominently on my desk, etc., but most importantly, I would often let team members know that I would be praying for them or a family member in need. Although some of them were not avidly praying themselves, they seemed to truly appreciate it.

Of course, for our respective holy days, I wished our Jewish team members a happy Chanukah, our Muslim team members Eid Mubarak, and our Christian team members a Merry Christmas. By hiring based on our shared values, our team was able to embrace and learn from each other and our respective religions. Because we didn't hide from our religious beliefs, we ended up with many team members who were willing to have discussions about their faith, inquisitive of others' beliefs, but also respectful of those uncomfortable with discussing it.

There are times in life when preaching the gospel requires words, and there are times when actions do as good, if not an even better, job. I'm a firm believer that in business ownership, actions almost always speak much louder than words.

Are you happy with your commitment to preach the Gospel with your actions? Would your team easily be able to identify your faith? Do they know that you pray for them?

Firefighters and Fire Inspectors

Throughout my career, I've observed that when the proverbial fire breaks out, there are firefighters and fire inspectors. There's a time and place for both, but the fire inspectors often get in the way of the firefighters. It's important to first put the fire out and then figure out how it started.

It's important to remember that, in most cases, just like real fires, proverbial fires are not started intentionally. If you hire the right people based on shared values, then you should never have to worry about intentional fires. The source of the fire typically boils down to one of two issues: people or process. So again, if you've hired the right people, then the default response we should have when a fire occurs is to determine what process failed and needs to be addressed.

It's been my experience that the fire inspectors who are always looking for an arsonist are the ones who prevent the emergency from being solved quickly. Put the fire out first, then, if necessary, figure out how it started and how to prevent it from occurring again.

Are you more inclined to be the fire inspector first rather than the firefighter? Are you able to identify the firefighters as opposed to the fire inspectors around you?

Overconfidence

One of my favorite core values is Humbly Confident. I believe that we should have a healthy level of confidence when operating in our God-given Unique Ability; after all, God gave us that ability for a reason. However, when working outside of our Unique Ability, we need to have the humility to ask questions and to learn from those who have more wisdom in a given area, especially for important items.

I've witnessed and been guilty of avoidable mistakes that were the result of overconfidence. Whether due to a false expectation that we are better than we are or, more often, a sense of insecurity that won't allow us to ask others for help for fear of exposing our lack of knowledge/expertise in a given area. Through conversations with other business owners as well as Hal Elrod's Miracle Mornings, I recognized the power of journaling to help me reframe my mindset every morning.

Looking back at the times in my life when my insecurities were at their highest, I sometimes came off as arrogant, which, I suppose, was just a mechanism to mask the insecurity. So, as we grew the business and interviewed or even hired team members who had moments of arrogance, we would attempt to make them feel secure. Half the time, the arrogance immediately subsided, and if it didn't, then we knew we had a problem with overconfidence and a bad core values match.

Where are you right now with your humility and your confidence? Do you feel that you could and should be speaking to someone about it? Do you feel that journaling will help?

Self-Limiting Beliefs

The largest hurdle that I likely faced, especially in the early days of the business, was my own self-limiting beliefs. I was fairly confident in my abilities, otherwise I never would've started the business. But as made clear several times throughout this book, my self-doubt and insecurities clearly informed my decisions for better or for worse.

My unconventional focus on not having any debt was clearly a result of my early struggles with financial responsibility. This made some things easier and some more of a challenge. Overall, the net result was very positive, in my opinion, but it's important to note that some of my team were very frustrated at times by my debt-free philosophy until I explained why. I likely should've explained the why sooner, especially to those most impacted by it.

Often, hiring decisions were impacted not for objective reasons but purely subjective. We might show on paper that we had more than enough work in the pipeline to bring on more team members, but something that occurred last month or even last year would give me an unjustifiable reason to delay or even hire a different person.

Are you fully aware of your self-limiting beliefs? As you think through your past, do you know which issues may hold you back? Do you know which ones may benefit you?

Strength of Kids

I recently had lunch with a friend of mine who was getting ready to start his own business. He had a lot of questions about the early days, how things are now, and what I would have done differently. He, rightfully, was very concerned about the impact starting his business would have on his family, both positive and negative. We talked a good bit about the sacrifices my kids had to make along the way. And the discussions I'm having with them now, about reaping the rewards of those sacrifices. He decided he would go home and talk to his wife and kids, especially his oldest daughter, who was ten years old, about his decision to start his own business, what that could mean for the family going forward, and what it would likely mean for the family right now. He reached out to me a few days later to tell me that he had spoken to his daughter, and she was so excited that her daddy was going to start his own business and was fully on board with whatever was needed from her.

A week later, he was talking with his daughter and said, "You haven't asked me for help with your math homework this week. We used to do your math homework together every day." She replied, "No, Daddy. I understand that you have to worry about the business. I will take care of my math, don't you worry." So, she had been doing her math homework on her own, and lo and behold, she had even brought her grades up by working so hard to make sure that her dad didn't have to worry about that.

Man, kids are so resilient. They really will help if they understand the mission and know that they're helping to impact their own and their family's future.

Who in your world are you "protecting" by not giving them the opportunity to step up and support your entrepreneurial journey in whatever way they can? Let your support system surprise you; I promise they will.

Who Not How®

I may have been able to reduce my time spent at work, as well as some of my self-limiting beliefs and insecurities had I learned earlier about the concept of Who Not How, as defined by Dan Sullivan and eloquently described by Ben Hardy.[13] At a basic level, Who Not How is a mindset for delegation and collaboration. Through delegation the entrepreneur finds someone, a who, to perform various tasks rather than learning how to do them. I try not to dwell on the amount of time and energy that I likely would've saved adapting this mindset earlier. I'm just glad that I eventually did.

Taking this a few steps further, Who Not How incorporates collaboration with other entrepreneurs to bring added value to the marketplace. Two entrepreneurs with an abundance mindset can come together and see how their individual strengths and the strengths of their organizations can complement each other and create new opportunities.

Who are the who's that you will need to address the how's that are not in your unique ability? How will you maintain a list of potential team members, vendors, and collaborators as you become aware of them along your journey?

From the Golf Course

Never a Reason to Swing a Golf Club 120 Percent

The first golf lesson I ever had was just a few years ago. The pro, giving me my lesson, very quickly advised me that there was never a reason to swing a golf club 120 percent. Every single swing I took, I swung out of my shoes to try to hit the ball as hard as I could. He pointed out that if I was trying to hit my eight iron 120 percent, I probably should just be swinging my seven iron or six iron instead. That made a lot of sense for my golf game, but I didn't think much about it afterward.

I recently had a good friend, Joe Apfelbaum, out on the practice range. He is a true visionary and phenomenal entrepreneur, currently on his third or fourth business but had never been golfing before. When I shared that tip with him, he looked at me and said, "Isn't that the same as business? If you're ever working at 120 percent, you're not using the right tools." So true. So well said and so succinct. As I reflect over the years, if I was operating at 120 percent, I either didn't have the right people in place, the right processes, or the right resources available. Whether swinging a golf club or working in business, going forward, I need to avoid operating at 120 percent.

What are you putting 120 percent effort into right now? Do you need new people, processes, or resources to get to 100 percent?

Faith Creates Confidence; Family Creates Humility

In that same conversation at the practice range, somehow, we also ended up on the topic of our Humbly Confident core value. While wreaking havoc on a few buckets of golf balls, we discussed some stories about business and some about our faith and our families, which then led us to the realization that "faith creates confidence; family creates humility."

During low moments of self-confidence, usually late at night, I've learned to turn to my faith in God. He has a plan for me, and if I do my best to look for signs of His plan and then use my time, talent, and treasure toward that plan, everything will turn out as He wants, not necessarily as I want. This strong faith has helped strengthen my confidence on many occasions. However, admittedly, I wasn't very good at this when I started the business. I've since learned to identify what *really* is the worst-case scenario and walk it back from there.

While our faith creates confidence, our family can help keep us humble. I'm not just talking about times like when Grace, our six-year-old daughter, asked me, "Why can't you be a normal daddy? Why do you always have to be a silly daddy?" I guess I was being too much on a Monday morning ride to school. I'm referring to the humility that hits the moment that your child is in your arms for the first time. The love that we feel for them, knowing that one of our biggest priorities just became their health and happiness. Or the humility that comes when you realize that no matter how hard you try, sometimes their health and safety are out of your control.

If I didn't have a strong faith to lean on, I may have put too much pressure on the success of the business. And if I didn't have the humility of a parent, I may have generated a sense of false pride. Our Humbly Confident core value was likely the one that benefited us the most.

Do you recognize the values that are core to you, knowing that you will want to and have to lean on them throughout your journey? They are going to be vital to your success.

Who are your Joe Apflebaums? Who are your friends that you can ideate with and speak about business, family, and faith with, all while having a few laughs?

Next Hole, New Hole

One day, I was golfing with my son, Gavin. I don't remember the exact circumstances of what happened on the hole, but safe to say he got a bogey or a double bogey. If you're not a fan of golf, just know he didn't get the score that he wanted to get on that hole. In golf, there are 18 holes, each hole has its own individual score that all adds up to the total score. The score for hole four has no numeric impact on the score for hole five but can have a significant mental impact, so you have to have a short memory. So, in trying to help him, and subsequently myself, with the mental game of golf, I repeated something to him that I had told him many times before: "Don't worry about this hole. The next hole is a new hole. Let's just move on." I wanted him to take the lessons he learned and move on, start the next hole with a blank slate, and go after it. What often happens, more for me than for my son, is that I shoot a bad score on one hole and let it get in my head, allowing it to impact the next five or six holes. I didn't think my supportive words landed great at the moment; however, on the next hole, he did really well. As I high-fived him, he said, "Next hole, new hole, right?" This became a mantra I would repeat to him whether golfing with him or dropping him off at a tournament: "Next hole, new hole."

Thinking back on that story, I've realized that "next hole, new hole" is a critical concept for business as well. The mindset to move on to the next one, take the lessons I learned, but start with a blank slate was very much needed. Throughout my career, and certainly throughout my entrepreneurial journey, some meetings with clients went well, and some didn't go well at all. Some interviews of new team members went well, and some didn't go well. You win some, you lose some. I had to be able to look at the wins and the losses, take the lessons learned, and move on. If I dwelled too much on what went wrong, I'd go down into a false sense of negativity, compounding the issue. Conversely, if after my wins, I was so full of myself, patting myself on the back for all the things I did great, and didn't look at what I could have done better, I could end up going into a false sense of positivity, leading towards an over-embellished self-confidence and an ego that would set me up for failure.

How good are you at the "next hole, new hole" mindset? What can you do to learn from, but also move on from, a bad meeting or interaction to avoid compounding the issue?

Every Entrepreneur Should Write a Book

The exercise of writing a book, even if it never gets published or sells a copy, has been well worth the time and effort. In writing this book, we've learned so much about ourselves, our team, and our business by looking back since the start, recalling some of the experiences, and having the benefit of knowing what worked and didn't work.

Reflecting on some of the business decisions that we made over the years with the benefit of knowing the end result has been very educational. Similarly, thinking about some of our team members' interviews and early days while knowing how much they would go on to accomplish has been eye-opening. On the other hand, seeing others that we were confident would be rock stars not live up to their potential has also resulted in some good reflection. Looking back at clients and projects that we missed out on or that we wanted to walk away from but didn't and later regretted has reinforced something we learned slowly: Sometimes, the best project is the one you don't get.

Similarly, this exercise caused us to see how our faith was intertwined in every aspect of our lives, including the business. Reflecting back, we can see that at the overwhelming times when things were really hairy, God sent us the support we needed. We just needed to open our eyes to see that the support was there and accept it.

Lastly, examining how our family has grown tremendously along this journey and has impacted us in so many amazing ways has ignited a new resolve for more ambitious ventures that incorporate them more deeply.

Going forward, we intend to write regularly about every business we start, even if the book is never published. We're confident that the learning in the moment will help us and the business grow tremendously. We hope you write one as well. When you do, let us know; we'd love to read it.

* * *

Wherever you are on your entrepreneurial journey, go out there and strengthen your Entrepreneurial Trinity. Remember that what we do is less important than how we do it. As stated by Fr. Daniel: "Any honest work can become the place of not only sanctification of self but also the restoration of the world. Any human endeavor taken on, inspired by love and animated by charity, has the capacity to renew and restore the world."[14]

As we stated at the start of the book, use our examples to learn from our mistakes and build on our knowledge. Don't let the setbacks discourage you. You can do it. We believe in you. And, in the words of Mary Jo, "You've got this. You're almost there." We'll be rooting for you and, more importantly, praying for you. We'll be here if you need us.

APPENDIX A: QUESTIONS TO ASK PRIOR TO THE JOURNEY

While writing this book, we created a list of questions that might have been beneficial for us to discuss before starting our entrepreneurial journey. We were reluctant to share it here because we didn't discuss these questions back then and, in some ways, benefited from the naivety of just putting our heads down and charging forward.

We are concerned that having this discussion is going to force guardrails onto a business that is likely very unpredictable at that point. However, if you are the type of couple that would benefit from having this discussion knowing that things will change and the guardrails should likely be somewhat loose, then keep reading:

1. How much time per week *should* we spend on the business?
2. How much time per week *should* we spend with family? On our faith? On our health?
3. How much revenue and profit do we **optimistically** expect the business to generate in year 1? Year 2? Year 3?
4. How much revenue and profit do we **realistically** expect the business to generate in year 1? Year 2? Year 3?
5. What are our top priorities?
6. What are our non-negotiables?
7. What *really* is the worst-case scenario?
8. How frequently do we want to communicate about the answers to these questions?

For a printable version of these questions, feel free to check out etrinitybook.com or scan the QR code below for a free download. We promise no contact info will be required to download.

APPENDIX B: QUESTIONS TO ASK ALONG THE JOURNEY

We created a list of questions to ask along the journey. These may be questions to reflect on at various stages along the journey.

Conception

Are you courageous enough to push yourself outside your comfort zone to help someone you care for be their best?

Who are the authors, mentors, and influencers that you are plugged into and gaining wisdom from?

Newborn

What is the realistic, worst-case scenario if your business doesn't succeed as you envision?

What does success look like to you?

Do you have a person in your support system who is willing to go above and beyond to help you succeed in the early days of your business?

How are you currently spending your time? Are you doing everything you *can* do or everything you *should* do?

What's your version of the newsletter? What are other low-cost, high-value methods that you can use to differentiate your new business from the competition?

Who is in your village?

Who motivates you to be a better person while simultaneously believing in you and pushing you to accomplish more in all aspects of life?

Who is the professional you have on such a high pedestal that you're nervous about reaching out to but are willing and eager to help if you just ask?

Who is your trusted peer who has already walked the road you're walking and has a positive but realistic view of what lies ahead? Who will tell you the Optimistic Truth and make you laugh when you need it?

Toddler Years

Who is in your circle is a great networker and is willing to invite you into their circle?

How frequently are you reading or listening to books and content that will help you along your path? How much of that time is devoted to business? Family? Faith?

Can you be the small "j" jerk that your business and your team need?

How do you view mistakes? Do you view them as learning moments? Are you comfortable sharing them with others?

Do you need help remembering to celebrate your wins? Who can you enlist, if necessary, to be your gauge and let you know when to celebrate them more frequently?

Is what you're reading and listening to diverse enough to cover all aspects of the Entrepreneurial Trinity? Where do you need to shift your focus more: faith, family, or business?

Adolescence

Who are your trusted friends/advisers who will help you make wise decisions when your emotions are conflicting with your own logic?

How many Free Days have you taken in the past year? What's preventing you from taking more? Who can assist you with taking more?

What resources will you use to develop the right operating system for your business? Have you found the one that resonates with you the most? Do you prefer a detailed business plan or a single sheet V/TO?

What is your Unique Ability? What is it you love doing that comes so effortlessly that you assume it's easy for everyone? Are you willing to lean into it? Are you willing to embrace your God-given talent?

Will your recruiting and hiring process allow you to find rockstars? What can you do to improve it?

Who is your finance guru? Who will you lean on for advice? Who will hold you accountable to ensure that you, the owner, are prioritizing your finances so that your budget includes all required expenses, including properly compensating yourself?

Are you comfortable being transparent with your team? With your clients? How transparent do you want to be?

Do you have an Executive Assistant?

Are you comfortable networking in large group settings or small ones? What types of events do you enjoy attending that you could consider replicating for your network? What can you do to add value to your network with no expectations of a return?

Do you know what your One Year From Today goal is? Do you need the help of other business leaders to help you clarify or strengthen it?

Are you comfortable being transparent with your team? With your clients? How transparent do you want to be?

Emerging Adulthood

Have I accomplished everything I wanted to with this venture? What's next for the business? Where do I want it to go? What's next for me? Where do I want to go? If I move on, will the company thrive without me?

How prepared are you for the inevitable emergency? What should you do to help your business survive? What should you do to protect your family?

What would you do if an interested buyer approached you about your business? Would you entertain their offer? Why?

Is your current faith community in line with your values? Is it challenging you to be the best version of yourself? Or is it simply good enough?

How would you define your generosity? Do you regularly push yourself outside your comfort zone?

What organizations are near you that your time, your money, and your heart will provide a great reward for others and an even bigger reward for you?

Adulthood

What is your heart beating for, and where are your steps taking you? Do you need some time to think it through? Are you being intentional with your time, talent, and treasure? Are you intentional with those you spend your time with?

Who is your ideal support system? Do you have your rock? Do you have mentors? How strong is your network? Should you reach out to a small business incubator in your area?

Are you and your spouse headed in the same direction but in separate cars? Are you being intentional about where you're driving your business? Your family? Your faith?

Unsolicited Advice

Are you doing enough verbally and non-verbally to show your gratitude to those sacrificing for you and your business?

Who are you comfortable speaking about your mental health with? Are you equally committed to getting the help you need, whether it is for your knee or your mind?

Where do you obtain your spiritual direction?

Are the religious leaders in your life pushing you enough and demanding the best of you? Do your friends inspire and motivate you? Would dedicated spiritual direction make sense for you?

Are you happy with your commitment to preach the Gospel with your actions? Would your team easily be able to identify your faith? Do they know that you pray for them?

Are you more inclined to be the fire inspector first rather than the firefighter? Are you able to identify the firefighters as opposed to the fire inspectors around you?

Where are you right now with your humility and your confidence? Do you feel that you could and should be speaking to someone about it? Do you feel that journaling will help?

Are you fully aware of your self-limiting beliefs? As you think through your past, do you know which issues may hold you back? Do you know which ones may benefit you?

Who in your world are you "protecting" by not giving them the opportunity to step up and support your entrepreneurial journey in whatever way they can?

Who are the who's that you will need to address the how's that are not in your unique ability? How will you maintain a list of potential team members, vendors, and collaborators as you become aware of them along your journey?

What are you putting 120 percent effort into right now? Do you need new people, processes, or resources to get to 100 percent?

Do you recognize the values that are core to you, knowing that you will want to and have to lean on them throughout your journey? They are going to be vital to your success.

Who are your friends that you can ideate with and speak about business, family, and faith with, all while having a few laughs?

How good are you at the "next hole, new hole" mindset? What can you do to learn from, but also move on from, a bad meeting or interaction to avoid compounding the issue?

APPENDIX C: ADDITIONAL RESOURCES

Business

To gain traction toward achieving your vision, visit EOSWorldwide.com

To learn more about Brian Sullivan as an EOS Implementer, visit EOSWorldwide.com/Brian-Sullivan

To learn more about Strategic Coach's business coaching for growth-minded entrepreneurs, visit StrategicCoach.com

To hear some of Dan Miller's wisdom on the *48 Days* podcast, visit 48Days.com/Category/48-Days-Podcast

Also, check out the What Drives You podcast with Kevin Miller: KevinMiller.co/Podcast

To learn more about EntreLeadership's proven way for business owners to lead a team, grow a business, and build a legacy, visit RamseySolutions.com/Business/Entreleadership

Family

To learn more about the ultimate planning retreat for high-achieving couples, visit G5Summit.com

To learn more about international adoption, visit HoltInternational.org

To learn more about the great work of Fr. Rick Frechette and the St. Luke Foundation for Haiti, please visit StLukeHaiti.org

To learn more about the great work of the Enfant Jesus Foundation in Haiti, please visit FondationEnfantJesus.org

To learn more about raising strong kids, visit MeekerParenting.com

Faith

To receive the daily mass readings via email, visit the US Council of Catholic Bishops website at Bible.USCCB.org/Daily-Bible-Reading#subscribe

To gain some wisdom and insight from Bishop Robert Barron, visit WordOnFire.org and subscribe to his daily reflections email at WordOnFire.org/Reflections

To help find God's peace through guided prayer and meditation, download the Hallow app or visit Hallow.com

To listen to the sermons of Fr. Daniel O'Mullane, visit OLMC.church/Livestream/#Homilies

To learn more about spiritual mentorship, visit SchoolOfFaith.com/Spiritual-Mentorship

To learn more about the great work of Catholic Charities in the US, visit CatholicCharitiesUSA.org

To learn more about Legatus, the international organization for Catholic business leaders, visit Legatus.org

To learn more about the Regnum Christi Federation's efforts to help people meet Jesus Christ, visit RegnumChristi.com

To learn more about Napa Institute's efforts to empower Catholic leaders to renew the Church and transform the culture, visit Napa-Institute.org

To learn more about the great Saint Padre Pio, visit the National Centre for Padre Pio at PadrePio.org

APPENDIX D: RECOMMENDED READING

Business

EntreLeadership: 20 Years of Practical Business Wisdom from the Trenches by Dave Ramsey

48 Days: To the Work You Love by Dan Miller

Traction: Get a Grip on Your Business by Gino Wickman

10x Is Easier Than 2x: How World-Class Entrepreneurs Achieve More by Doing Less by Dan Sullivan and Dr. Benjamin Hardy

> Also: *Who Not How: The Formula to Achieve Bigger Goals Through Accelerating Teamwork* by Dan Sullivan and Dr. Benjamin Hardy
>
> *Also: The 4 C's Formula: Your building blocks of growth: commitment, courage, capability, and confidence* by Dan Sullivan

Good to Great: Why Some Companies Make the Leap...And Others Don't by Jim Collins

The Five Dysfunctions of a Team: A Leadership Fable by Patrick Lencioni

High Energy Networking: Get anything you want in life while building meaningful relationships that last a lifetime by Joe Apfelbaum

From Strength to Strength: Finding Success, Happiness, and Deep Purpose in the Second Half of Life by Arthur C. Brooks

The Emigrant Edge: How to Make It Big in America by Brian Buffini

Business Secrets from the Bible: Spiritual Success Strategies for Financial Abundance by Rabbi Daniel Lappin

Faith

Haiti: The God of Tough Places, the Lord of Burnt Men by Fr. Richard Frechette

Tuesdays with Morrie: An Old Man, a Young Man, and Life's Greatest Lesson by Mitch Albom

> Also: *Finding Chika: A Little Girl, an Earthquake, and the Making of a Family* by Mitch Albom

I Am With You: Lessons of Hope and Courage in Times of Crisis by Cardinal Timothy M. Dolan

Rebuilt: The Story of a Catholic Parish: Awakening the Faithful, Reaching the Lost, and Making Church Matter by Fr. Michael White and Tom Corcoran

Ordinary Time: Finding Holiness in Everyday Life by Fr. Mike Schmitz

Suffering Changes Everything by Fr. Jorge Obregón and Nayeli Pereznegrón

To Light a Fire on the Earth: Proclaiming the Gospel in a Secular Age by Bishop Robert Barron

> Also: *Catholicism: A Journey to the Heart of the Faith* by Bishop Robert Barron

Pray, Hope, and Don't Worry: True Stories of Padre Pio by Diane Allen

Francis of Assisi: The Life by Augustine Thompson

Too Small a World: The Life of Mother Frances Cabrini by Theodore Maynard

Family

Total Money Makeover Updated and Expanded: A Proven Plan for Financial Peace by Dave Ramsey

> Also: *Smart Money Smart Kids: Raising the Next Generation to Win with Money* by Dave Ramsey and Rachel Cruze

Raising Grateful Kids in an Entitled World: How One Family Learned That Saying No Can Lead to Life's Biggest Yes by Kristen Welch

Boys Should Be Boys: 7 Secrets to Raising Healthy Sons by Meg Meeker

Also: *Strong Fathers, Strong Daughters: 10 Secrets Every Father Should Know* by Meg Meeker

Wisdom of Our Fathers: Lessons and Letters from Daughters and Sons by Tim Russert

The Purpose Driven Life: What on Earth Am I Here For? by Rick Warren

Make Your Bed: Little Things That Can Change Your Life...And Maybe the World by Admiral William H. McRaven

The 3 Big Questions for a Frantic Family: A Leadership Fable...About Restoring Sanity to the Most Important Organization in Your Life by Patrick Lencioni

The Promise of a Pencil: How an Ordinary Person Can Create Extraordinary Change by Adam Braun

Trusted: Preparing Your Kids for a Lifetime of God-Honoring Money Management by Matt Bell

Leverage: Using Temporal Wealth for Eternal Gain by Kenneth Boa

ENDNOTES

1 Brian Buffini, *The Emigrant Edge: How To Make It Big in America* (New York, NY: Howard Books, 2017).

2 Simon Sinek, "How Great Leaders Inspire Action," Simon Sinek: How great leaders inspire action | TED Talk, September 2009, https://www.ted.com/talks/simon_sinek_how_great_leaders_inspire_action/transcript.

3 Patrick Lencioni, "The jerk Factor," The Table Group, January 2015, https://www.tablegroup.com/the-jerk-factor/.

4 Patrick Lencioni, host, "Open on Sunday with Craig Groeschel." At the Table (podcast), March 7, 2024. https://www.tablegroup.com/217-open-on-sunday-with-craig-groeschel/

5 Stephen R. Covey, A. Roger Merrill, and Rebecca R. Merrill, First Things First (New York, NY: Free Press, 1996).

6 Dan Sullivan, The Gap and the Gain (Carlsbad, CA: Hay House Business, 2021).

7 Dan Sullivan, The 4 C's Formula (Toronto, Ontario: Strategic Coach Inc., 2015).

8 Keith Ferrazzi and Tahl Raz, Never Eat Alone: And Other Secrets to Success, One Relationship at a Time (New York, NY: Crown, 2023).

9 Roger Thompson, "Reimagining the Mba," Harvard Business School Alumni, December 1, 2011, https://www.alumni.hbs.edu/stories/Pages/story-bulletin.aspx?num=1024.

10 Rabbi Daniel Lapin, *Business Secrets from the Bible: Spiritual Success Strategies for Financial Abundance* (Hoboken, NJ: John Wiley & Sons, Inc., 2014).

11 Kenneth Boa, *Leverage: Using Temporal Wealth for Eternal Gain* (Trinity House Publishers, 2023).

12 Arthur C. Brooks, *From Strength to Strength* (BLOOMSBURY PUBLISHING PLC, 2022).

13 Dan Sullivan and Benjamin Hardy, *Who Not How: The Formula to Achieve Bigger Goals through Accelerating Teamwork* (Carlsbad, CA: Hay House, Inc., 2020).

14 Fr. Daniel, "Wednesday of the Fifth Week of Easter," Father Daniel's Homilies, May 1, 2024, https://www.podbean.com/ep/pb-8xcmh-15fe6da.

ACKNOWLEDGMENTS

Our journey has been our greatest treasure. Getting to sit side by side for the past year and put 20 years' worth of memories and miracles on paper has been the gift of a lifetime. To all of our friends and family, as well as the passersby who've jumped in our boat along the way and taken up an oar, we are eternally grateful.

Thank you particularly:

~Dad (Pat Sullivan) - for setting the example of what tireless dedication to God and family truly looks like.

~The Sullivan Engineering Team - for believing in the vision and your dedication to create a work environment unmatched anywhere else.

~Fr. Daniel O'Mullane and the OLMC family - for challenging us spiritually and pushing us beyond our comfort to answer God's call.

~Fr. Rick Frechette - for leading a life that inspires us to be better disciples of Jesus, you are the epitome of a modern-day hero and living saint.

~Dr. Hourani - for seeing in me what I couldn't see in myself; your life and vocation are an inspiration to all.

~Mark O'Donnell - for helping our team accomplish our vision while pushing me to be a better leader, father, and husband.

~The Igniting Souls team, especially Travis White and Jill Ellis, for sharing your editing and publishing expertise to help us get the vision of this book across the finish line.

ABOUT THE AUTHORS

Brian and Mary Jo are devout Catholics, proud parents of seven, and entrepreneurs. They are dedicated to helping other entrepreneurial couples understand the value of prioritizing their family and their faith. Through their first book, *Entrepreneurial Trinity*, Brian and Mary Jo humbly share their successes and struggles along their journey to help others who have started or are starting their first business.

In 2010, they launched their first business, focused on providing great services, with fantastic people that shared similar values. Through a great deal of hard work, determination, and incredible support from each other, they survived the early startup days and steadily grew the team. That team grew so rapidly that they earned a spot on the Inc. 5000 list for five straight years from 2017 through 2021.

As a family, they enjoy volunteering for and supporting causes near to their heart, including a local food pantry, their children's Catholic schools, and various schools and hospitals in Haiti.

To spend more time as a family and pursue new opportunities, following God's plan for their lives, Brian and Mary Jo sold Sullivan Engineering in 2021.

Connect with Brian and Mary Jo at EntrepreneurialTrinity.com

CONNECT WITH BRIAN & MARY JO

Follow them on LinkedIn today.

LinkedIn.com/in/BrianSullivanEngineer

LinkedIn.com/in/Mary-Jo-Sullivan

EOS
ENTREPRENEURIAL
OPERATING SYSTEM

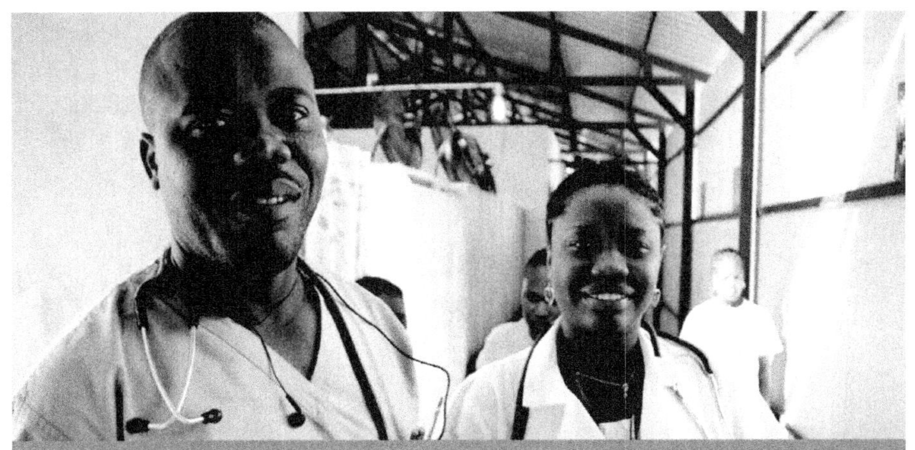

ST. LUKE
FOUNDATION
FOR HAITI

Printed in Great Britain
by Amazon